THE
WHITEBOARD
BIBLE®

VOLUME 3

THE
CHURCH
and
JESUS'
RETURN

Allen Jackson

PASTOR, WORLD OUTREACH CHURCH

allenjackson.com

© 2015 by Allen Jackson for *The Whiteboard Bible Vol. 3: The Church and Jesus' Return*. First edition 2014. Revised edition 2015.

The Whiteboard Bible® by Allen Jackson Ministries

Published by Allen Jackson Ministries
1921 New Salem Road, Hwy. 99
Murfreesboro, TN 37128

Special Sales:
Most Allen Jackson Ministries books are available at special quantity discounts when purchased in bulk by corporations, organizations, and special-interest groups. Custom imprinting or excerpting can also be done to fit special needs. For more information, please email: contact@allenjackson.com.

Illustrations: Imago
Design: Tommy Owen

ISBN: 978-1-61718-031-6

THE WHITEBOARD BIBLE

THE CHURCH and JESUS' RETURN

CONTENTS

APPENDIX

SMALL GROUP LEADERS

ABOUT THE AUTHOR

INTRODUCTION

The Bible is a collection of sixty-six books. Many different authors contributed to the work. It was written in different cultural settings over a period of hundreds of years. The books are not arranged in chronological order. The names seem unusual, and the places are mostly unknown. It is not surprising that most Christians do not understand the Bible. We typically settle for a verse that offers comfort or hope and imagine that in a handful of verses we have the essence of this remarkable book.

The Bible tells a story. The amazing narrative begins with creation and concludes with Jesus triumphant. Between Genesis and Revelation is the story of God's interaction with the descendants of Adam. The Bible is not intended to be a science book or a history book. It is possible to gain historical insight from reading the Bible and even to understand our world better. The primary objective is to provide the reader insight into Almighty God and His interactions with the descendants of Adam.

Often we avoid reading the Bible, thinking it is simply too complex or boring. *The Whiteboard Bible* study has been designed to help anyone gain a fundamental understanding of the narrative of the Bible. Inside the books of the Bible are amazing accounts of men and women whose lives were transformed by God. The Bible unfolds a revelation of God that invites all readers toward hope and purpose.

Through three volumes we will develop a twelve-point timeline that will serve as the framework for all the characters and events in the Bible. We will take a journey from creation through the emergence of the Hebrew people. We will hear the prophets and listen to the Sadducees challenge Jesus. By the time the study is complete we will be able to recount the progression of the biblical events in a simple, sequential order.

In this third volume we will consider the New

Testament and the fulfillment of so many of God's promises in Jesus. We will begin with the Gospels— the Jesus-story—continue through the book of Acts—the emerging Church—and finally move to the book of Revelation—the promise of Jesus' return.

The Bible is not beyond knowing. If you will invest as little as ten minutes a day in reading through your Bible, in the course of one year you can read through this amazing book. The expression of this small discipline can change your life.

Allen Jackson

OUTLINE OF EACH SESSION

A typical group session for *The Whiteboard Bible* will include the following:

GETTING STARTED. The foundation for spiritual growth is an intimate connection with God and His family. A few people who really know you and who earn your trust provide a place to experience the life Jesus invites you to live. Using the icebreaker questions enables you to connect with one or two in your group to begin the discussion with ease.

DVD TEACHING SEGMENT. Serving as a companion to *The Whiteboard Bible* small group study guide is *The Whiteboard Bible* video teaching. This DVD is designed to present unique illustrations from the whiteboard and helpful teaching segments from Pastor Allen Jackson.

DISCUSSION. This section is where you will process as a group the teaching from the DVD. We want to help you apply the insights from Scripture practically, creatively, and from your heart as well as your head. Allowing the timeless truths from God's Word to transform our lives in Christ is our greatest aim.

APPLICATION. The objective of Bible study is not primarily information but transformation. Each week we will walk through questions intended to help us not only to learn but to apply what we have learned to our daily life.

DEEPER BIBLE STUDY. If you have time and want to dig deeper into more Bible passages about the topic at hand, we've provided additional passages and questions. Your group may choose to do homework after of each meeting in order to cover more biblical material. If you prefer not to do homework, the Going Deeper section will provide you with plenty to discuss within the group. These options allow individuals or the whole group to expand their study, while still accommodating those who can't do homework or are new to your group.

DAILY DEVOTIONALS. Each week on the Daily Devotionals pages we provide Scriptures to read and reflect on between group meetings. We suggest you use this section to seek God on your own throughout the week. This time at home should begin and end with prayer. Don't get in a hurry; take enough time to hear God's direction.

WEEKLY MEMORY VERSES. For each session we have provided a Memory Verse that emphasizes an important truth from the session. Memorizing Scripture can be a vital part of filling our minds with God's will for our lives. We encourage you to give this important habit a try.

READ ALOUD. Inside the Application and Discussion sections are additional teaching components to use with your group. These sections are a natural way to set up more dialogue for the questions that follow and also serve as a great tool for opening discussion in your group.

WEEK 1

INTRODUCTION

Welcome to *The Whiteboard Bible*, a way of learning God's Word that enables us to understand the story of the Bible and not just a collection of Bible stories. As we begin volume three, our focus will turn to Jesus, His life, and His ministry. The New Testament does not begin a new story. It provides a fulfillment of the journey we began in Genesis. Abraham looked forward to the day of Jesus. King David anticipated Jesus' story. The prophets, with great anticipation, spoke of the Messiah.

JESUS' BIRTH and DEATH

These six sessions will guide you through the most remarkable segment of human history. Almighty God, the Creator of all things, sent His Son to dwell among us. It is the fulfillment of a promise God made in the first chapters of Genesis. Take a little time each week to review the timeline. The points along this chronological map will help organize the familiar names and events in sequential order. The powerful drama of God and people will emerge in a more personal way as the Bible becomes a coherent series of events and not just a collection of random activities and mystical figures from the past. Almighty God has a purpose for each life. Recognizing the epic panorama of Scripture will add momentum to your journey.

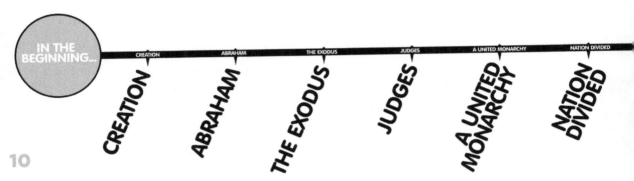

THE CHURCH

IN THE BEGINNING...

CREATION · ABRAHAM · THE EXODUS · JUDGES · A UNITED MONARCHY · NATION DIVIDED

CREATION

ABRAHAM

THE EXODUS

JUDGES

A UNITED MONARCHY

NATION DIVIDED

10

THE **WHITEBOARD** BIBLE

GETTING STARTED

Begin the session with a question below or brief activity to become better acquainted with one another.

1 At Christmas we remember and celebrate Jesus' birth. Which character in the nativity scene would you most like to interview and why?

2 At Easter we remember and celebrate Jesus' death and resurrection. Share an Easter tradition for your family.

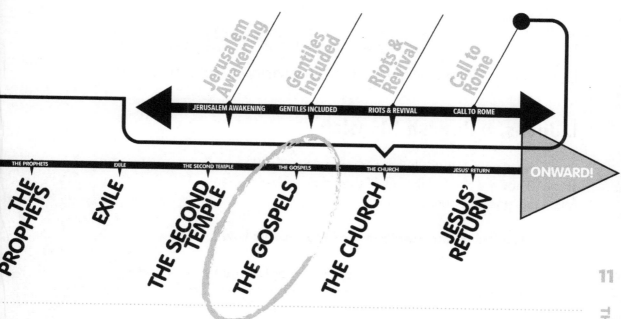

11

OUTLINE OF DVD LESSON

Use the outline below to follow along during the DVD.

I. Jesus, a Jewish Messiah

The Gospels are not the beginning of a "new faith" or a "new story." They are the fulfillment of the story we have been following since Genesis.

A. Jesus Is the Fulfillment of the Mosaic Law

Matthew 5:17-18

17 "Do not think that I have come to abolish the Law or the Prophets; I have not come to abolish them but to fulfill them. 18 I tell you the truth, until heaven and earth disappear, not the smallest letter, not the least stroke of a pen, will by any means disappear from the Law until everything is accomplished."

Romans 10:4

Christ is the end of the law so that there may be righteousness for everyone who believes.

B. The Jewish People Did Not Fail

Romans 9:4-5

4 The people of Israel. Theirs is the adoption as sons; theirs the divine glory, the covenants, the receiving of the law, the temple worship and the promises. 5 Theirs are the patriarchs, and from them is traced the human ancestry of Christ, who is God over all, forever praised! Amen.

1. They delivered a Messiah.
2. They gave us the prophets.
3. They gave us the Scriptures.
4. They gave us the covenants.

C. The New Jerusalem

Revelation 21:12

It had a great, high wall with twelve gates, and with twelve angels at the gates. On the gates were written the names of the twelve tribes of Israel.

II. Jesus' Birth and Death Are the Essential Aspects

A. Jesus' Birth—The Incarnation
Luke 1:30-33

[30] But the angel said to her, "Do not be afraid, Mary, you have found favor with God. [31] You will be with child and give birth to a son, and you are to give him the name Jesus. [32] He will be great and will be called the Son of the Most High. The Lord God will give him the throne of his father David, [33] and he will reign over the house of Jacob forever; his kingdom will never end."

John 1:14

The Word became flesh and made his dwelling among us. We have seen his glory, the glory of the One and Only, who came from the Father, full of grace and truth.

B. Jesus' Death—The Crucifixion and Resurrection
1. Condemned to death by Pilate, the Roman governor
John 19:19

Pilate had a notice prepared and fastened to the cross. It read: JESUS OF NAZARETH, THE KING OF THE JEWS.

2. Raised to life again
Luke 24:11-12

[11] But they did not believe the women, because their words seemed to them like nonsense. [12] Peter, however, got up and ran to the tomb. Bending over, he saw the strips of linen lying by themselves, and he went away, wondering to himself what had happened.

C. Redemption
2 Corinthians 5:21

God made him who had no sin to be sin for us, so that in him we might become the righteousness of God.

God, I am a sinner and I need a Savior. I believe Jesus of Nazareth is your Son. Forgive me of my sins. I forgive all who have sinned against me. Jesus, be Lord of my life. I want to serve you—be Lord of all that I am and all that I have. Thank you for accepting me into you Kingdom. In Jesus name, amen.

THE WHITEBOARD BIBLE

A Mighty Source
THE BIRTH & DEATH OF JESUS

JESUS: MOST WIDELY KNOWN HUMAN IN HISTORY

PEOPLE LEARN ABOUT HIM AT ALL DIFFERENT AGES

FAME-OMETER

JESUS

MADONNA · JUSTIN BIEBER · GEO WASHINGTON · GENGHIS KHAN · LEBRON JAMES · WALDO · MICHAEL JORDAN · TIGER · TIGGER

OOOH - I KNOW THE ANSWER TO THIS ONE

MOST ARE FAMILIAR WITH HIS BIRTH & DEATH: IS IT BECAUSE EVERYBODY IS BORN & DIES?

OR BECAUSE JESUS' BIRTH & DEATH WERE MIRACULOUS?

HAPPY 40TH HON

THAT'S AN OXYMORON

SAY THAT AGAIN AND IT'S YOUR FUNERAL

A LIFE FULL OF MIRACLES: FROM HIS BIRTH...

BORN OF A PREGNANT VIRGIN

THAT'S NEVER HAPPENED BEFORE

..THROUGH HIS LIFE...

PICK UP YOUR MAT & GO HOME!

WOW

MAYBE HE IS THE MESSIAH WHO WILL OVERTHROW ROME

WELL - YOU'RE HALF RIGHT

THE CHURCH

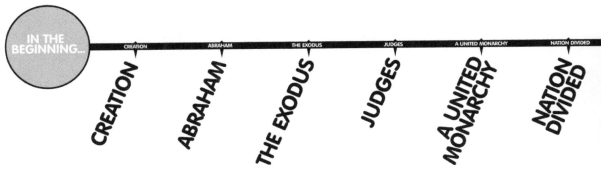

IN THE BEGINNING...

CREATION · ABRAHAM · THE EXODUS · JUDGES · A UNITED MONARCHY · NATION DIVIDED

CREATION · **ABRAHAM** · **THE EXODUS** · **JUDGES** · **A UNITED MONARCHY** · **NATION DIVIDED**

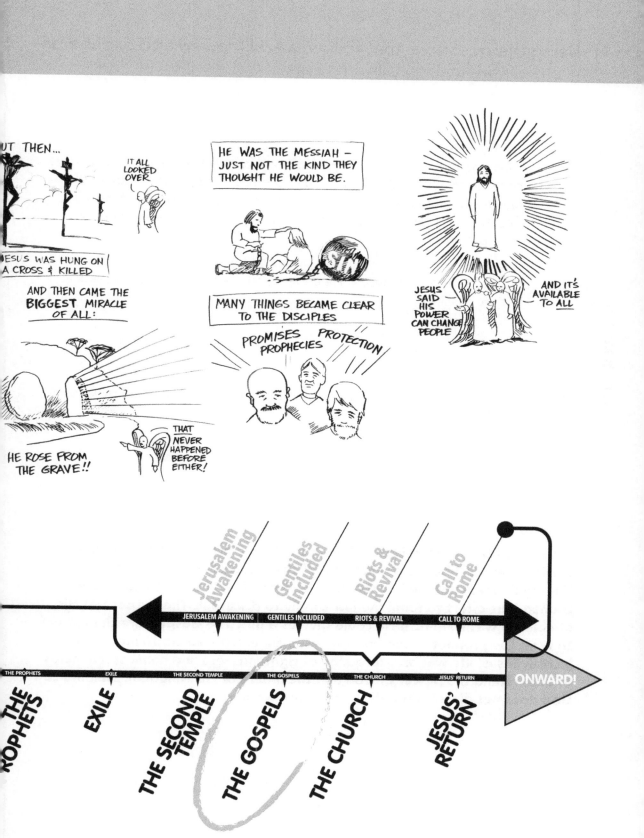

DISCUSSION

Using the questions that follow, we will review and expand on the teaching we just experienced.

Matthew 5:17-18

17 "Do not think that I have come to abolish the Law or the prophets; I have not come to abolish them but to fulfill them. 18 I tell you the truth, until heaven and earth disappear, not the smallest letter, not the least stroke of a pen, will by any means disappear from the Law until everything is accomplished."

1 Jesus is our model. How did He understand the Law and the prophets to relate to His life?

2 If the Law and the prophets were important to Jesus, how should we view them?

READ ALOUD

Jesus was born into a religious Jewish family. He grew up to be an observant Jewish man. His life was a fulfillment of the Mosaic Law. Jesus fully met the requirements of the law for righteousness. It is illogical to make the tremendous effort to fulfill the law simply to discard it. The purpose of His obedience was so in turn He could give us a gift. The Gospels are the answer to what the prophets cried out for. Jesus demonstrated God's mercy and justice. Jesus' life was an expression of righteousness and holiness. He helps us understand the power of God and the nature of His Kingdom. Yielding to God does not diminish our lives; it is empowering!

Romans 9:4-5

⁴ The people of Israel. Theirs is the adoption as sons; theirs the divine glory, the covenants, the receiving of the law, the temple worship and the promises. ⁵ Theirs are the patriarchs, and from them is traced the human ancestry of Christ, who is God over all, forever praised! Amen.

3 Paul reminded us that we are indebted to the Jewish people. List three or four things we have received through the faithfulness of the Jewish people.

4 Being the people of God takes courage. Moses, Joshua, David, and Daniel each demonstrated tremendous strength and courage. Which Old Testament character's courage is most remarkable to you? Why?

READ ALOUD

The Bible is a very personal book. God consistently demonstrates an interest in the well-being of His people. The account of Jesus' birth is a very personal account as well.

Luke 1:30-33

30 But the angel said to her, "Do not be afraid, Mary, you have found favor with God. 31 You will be with child and give birth to a son, and you are to give him the name Jesus. 32 He will be great and will be called the Son of the Most High. The Lord God will give him the throne of his father David, 33 and he will reign over the house of Jacob forever; his kingdom will never end."

5 What is the angel's first instruction to Mary?

6 "Favor with God" brought tremendous change to Mary's life plan. Describe how the angelic visit may have changed Mary's dreams.

John 18:36-37

36 Jesus said, "My kingdom is not of this world. If it were, my servants would fight to prevent my arrest by the Jews. But now my kingdom is from another place." 37 "You are a king, then!" said Pilate. Jesus answered, "You are right in saying I am a king. In fact, for this reason I was born, and for this I came into the world, to testify to the truth. Everyone on the side of truth listens to me."

7 Why was Jesus' statement about being a king important?

AND THEN CAME THE
BIGGEST MIRACLE
OF ALL:

HE ROSE FROM
THE GRAVE!!

APPLICATION

Now it's time to make some personal applications of all we've been thinking about in the last few minutes.

READ ALOUD

What you choose to believe about Jesus is very important. You may believe He was an actual historical figure, a good man, a prophet, or even a miracle worker. If you take the step of faith to believe Jesus is the Son of God, then you must decide if you will accept Him as Lord and serve Him as King. Church membership does not draw the line of demarcation for time and eternity; your decisions regarding Jesus will.

8 Why are the circumstances of Jesus' birth important?

Romans 10:9-10

⁹ That if you confess with your mouth, "Jesus is Lord," and believe in your heart that God raised him from the dead, you will be saved. ¹⁰ For it is with your heart that you believe and are justified, and it is with your mouth that you confess and are saved.

9 Jesus' redemptive work—His death and resurrection—make freedom possible for us. How do we appropriate this freedom?

READ ALOUD

It takes courage to follow Jesus—courage to acknowledge our own sin and failure, courage to yield our lives to the lordship of Jesus, and courage to choose God's will. However, the benefits are truly unequaled.

Matthew 11:28-29

28 "Come to me, all you who are weary and burdened, and I will give you rest. 29 Take my yoke upon you and learn from me, for I am gentle and humble in heart, and you will find rest for your souls."

10 Describe the time when you chose to acknowledge Jesus as Lord and King. How did other opinions impact your decision?

11 How have you experienced new freedoms since choosing Jesus as Lord?

PRAYER

Close the session in prayer. Share prayer requests with the group, and pray for each other. Close by praying the following prayer together.

Heavenly Father, I am a sinner, and I need a Savior. I believe Jesus of Nazareth is Your Son. Forgive me of my sins. I forgive all who have sinned against me. Jesus, be Lord of my life. I want to serve You; be Lord of all that I am and all that I have. Thank You for accepting me into Your Kingdom. In Jesus' name, amen.

Prayer requests this week:

GOING DEEPER

This section is designed to do as homework, if you choose, between your Small Group meetings.

Jesus Fulfilled the Mosaic Law

Jesus' birth, death, and resurrection are the fulfillments of the story we have been reading since Genesis. In no way do we discard the Old Testament but embrace it as Jesus did: not to abolish the law or prophets but to fulfill them. The Old Testament prophets looked forward to the day of Christ's appearing on earth.

Let's look at a few Scriptures in the Old Testament that tell of the coming Christ and the New Testament Scriptures that speak of their fulfillment.

Jesus Born of a Virgin

Isaiah 7:14

Therefore the Lord himself will give you a sign: The virgin will be with child and will give birth to a son, and will call him Immanuel.

Matthew 1:22-23

22 All this took place to fulfill what the Lord had said through the prophet: 23 "The virgin will be with child and will give birth to a son, and they will call him Immanuel" (which means "God with us.")

Jesus Will Be in Abraham's Family Tree

Genesis 22:18

"And through your offspring all nations on earth will be blessed, because you have obeyed me."

Matthew 1:1

A record of the genealogy of Jesus Christ, the son of David, the son of Abraham.

Jesus Teaches in Parables

Psalm 78:2-4

2 I will open my mouth in parables; I will utter hidden things, things from of old—3 what we have heard and known, what our fathers have told us. 4 We will not hide them from our children; we will tell the next generation the praiseworthy deeds of the LORD, his power, and the wonders he has done.

Matthew 13:34-35
³⁴ *Jesus spoke all these things to the crowd in parables; he did not say anything to them without using a parable.* ³⁵ *So was fulfilled what was spoken through the prophet: "I will open my mouth in parables, I will utter things hidden since the creation of the world."*

Jesus a Suffering Savior

Isaiah 53:5-6
⁵ *But he was pierced for our transgressions, he was crushed for our iniquities; the punishment that brought us peace was upon him, and by his wounds we are healed.* ⁶ *We all, like sheep, have gone astray, each of us has turned to his own way; and the LORD has laid on him the iniquity of us all.*

The New Testament understands Jesus as the fulfillment of many Old Testament prophecies. Let's consider what the New Testament anticipates for our lives.

Revelation 21:1-4
¹ *Then I saw a new heaven and a new earth, for the first heaven and the first earth had passed away, and there was no longer any sea.* ² *I saw the Holy City, the new Jerusalem, coming down out of heaven from God, prepared as a bride beautifully dressed for her husband.* ³ *And I heard a loud voice from the throne saying, "Now the dwelling of God is with men, and he will live with them. They will be his people, and God himself will be with them and be their God.* ⁴ *He will wipe every tear from their eyes. There will be no more death or mourning or crying or pain, for the old order of things has passed away."*

- List three or four things that we can anticipate for our future.

1 John 1:9
If we confess our sins, he is faithful and just and will forgive us our sins and purify us from all unrighteousness.

- If you confess your sins, what will God do for you?

25

THE WHITEBOARD BIBLE

John 16:7

"But I tell you the truth: It is for your good that I am going away. Unless I go away, the Counselor will not come to you; but if I go, I will send him to you.

- What did Jesus say He would do? In what ways do you cooperate with the Holy Spirit?

John 14:3

"And if I go and prepare a place for you, I will come back and take you to be with me that you also may be where I am."

- What does Jesus say He is preparing for us? What does He promise to do?

MANY THINGS BECAME CLEAR TO THE DISCIPLES
PROMISES
PROTECTION
PROPHECIES

DAILY REFLECTIONS

These are daily reviews of the key Bible verses and related others that will help you think about and apply the insights from this session.

DAY 1

Luke 1:28

Greetings

The angel went to her and said, "Greetings, you who are highly favored! The Lord is with you."

Reflection Question:
Do you live your life with the expectation of God's favor? What would you do differently if you were assured of His presence in your situations?

DAY 2

Luke 1:36-37

Believe

36 "Even Elizabeth your relative is going to have a child in her old age, and she who was said to be barren is in her sixth month. 37 For nothing is impossible with God."

Reflection Question:
Why do you think the angel told Mary about Elizabeth? Does God's Word assure you protection for the impossible situations in your life?

DAY 3

Luke 23:28

Concern

Jesus turned and said to them, "Daughters of Jerusalem, do not weep for me; weep for yourselves and for your children."

Reflection Question:
What are you weeping for today?

DAY 4

Luke 24:6-7

He is Risen

⁶ "He is not here; he has risen! Remember how he told you, while he was still with you in Galilee: ⁷ 'The Son of Man must be delivered into the hands of sinful men, be crucified and on the third day be raised again.'"

Reflection Question:
Do you ever forget what God's Word has told you about your situations?

_____

_____

_____

_____

_____

_____

DAY 5

Luke 24:46

Promotion

He said to them, "This is what is written: The Christ will suffer and rise from the dead on the third day."

Reflection Question:
Does a warning of difficulty help or hinder you?

_____

_____

_____

_____

_____

_____

WEEKLY MEMORY VERSE

⁶ HE IS NOT HERE; HE HAS RISEN! REMEMBER HOW HE TOLD YOU, WHILE HE WAS STILL WITH YOU IN GALILEE: ⁷ THE SON OF MAN MUST BE DELIVERED INTO THE HANDS OF SINFUL MEN, BE CRUCIFIED AND ON THE THIRD DAY BE RAISED AGAIN."

LUKE 24:6-7

WEEK 2

INTRODUCTION

The city of Jerusalem is a location God has chosen for Himself. This is a remarkable fact. Of all the cities in the world, there is one that is central to the purposes of God in the earth. Jerusalem is a desert city—hot and dusty. It is not located on a major waterway or a main highway; Jerusalem is tucked away in the Judean hills. By most standards it is a very unremarkable place—except God has chosen Jerusalem as an essential element in His plan.

JERUSALEM AWAKENING

Abraham was directed to take his son Isaac and offer a sacrifice on Mount Moriah. Even before the city of Jerusalem was established, God was directing His purposes through this place. This same mountaintop was purchased by King David to be the site for the temple. Jesus was arrested, crucified, and resurrected in Jerusalem. It is not surprising that the Church was launched through an awakening of the city of Jerusalem.

Psalm 122:6
Pray for the peace of Jerusalem: "May those who love you be secure."

Zechariah 12:2-3
2 "I am going to make Jerusalem a cup that sends all the surrounding peoples reeling. Judah will be besieged as well as Jerusalem. 3 On that day, when all the nations of the earth are gathered against her, I will make Jerusalem an immovable rock for all the nations. All who try to move it will injure themselves."

THE CHURCH

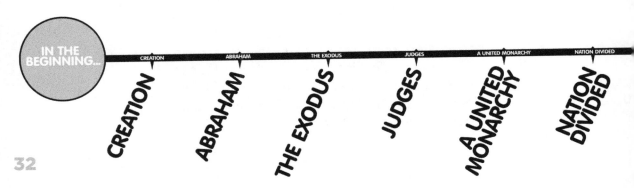

IN THE BEGINNING...

CREATION   ABRAHAM   THE EXODUS   JUDGES   A UNITED MONARCHY   NATION DIVIDED

CREATION

ABRAHAM

THE EXODUS

JUDGES

A UNITED MONARCHY

NATION DIVIDED

GETTING STARTED

Begin the session with a question below or brief activity to become better acquainted with one another.

1 For anyone in the group who has visited Jerusalem, what is your most treasured memory?

2 When was Jerusalem last mentioned in the news? Why?

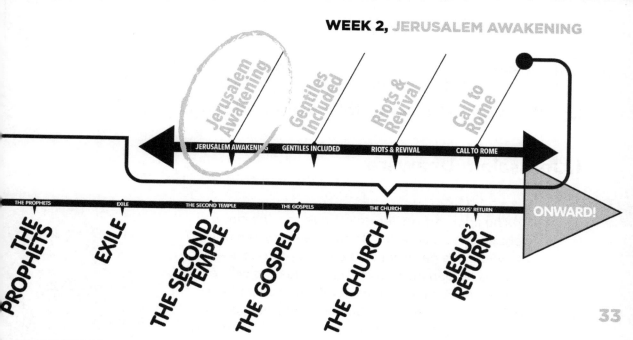

OUTLINE OF DVD LESSON

Use the outline below to follow along during the DVD.

I. Jerusalem Unaware

Luke 19:41-44

[41] As he approached Jerusalem and saw the city, he wept over it [42] and said, "If you, even you, had only known on this day what would bring you peace—but now it is hidden from your eyes. [43] The days will come upon you when your enemies will build an embankment against you and encircle you and hem you in on every side. [44] They will dash you to the ground, you and the children within your walls. They will not leave one stone on another, because you did not recognize the time of God's coming to you."

II. Jerusalem Awakening

Acts 2:36-41

[36] "Therefore let all Israel be assured of this: God has made this Jesus, whom you crucified, both Lord and Christ." [37] When the people heard this, they were cut to the heart and said to Peter and the other apostles, "Brothers, what shall we do?" [38] Peter replied, "Repent and be baptized, every one of you, in the name of Jesus Christ for the forgiveness of your sins. And you will receive the gift of the Holy Spirit. [39] The promise is for you and your children and for all who are far off—for all whom the Lord our God will call." [40] With many other words he warned them; and he pleaded with them, "Save yourselves from this corrupt generation." [41] Those who accepted his message were baptized, and about three thousand were added to their number that day.

III. Person and Work of the Holy Spirit

John 16:12-13

[12] "I have much more to say to you, more than you can now bear. [13] But when he, the Spirit of truth, comes, he will guide you into all truth."

A. Miraculous

Acts 3:6-8

[6] Then Peter said, "Silver or gold I do not have, but what I have I give you. In the name of Jesus Christ of Nazareth, walk." [7] Taking him by the right hand, he helped him up, and instantly the man's feet and ankles became strong. [8] He jumped to his feet and began to walk. Then he went with them into the temple courts, walking and jumping, and praising God.

Acts 5:14-16

[14] Nevertheless, more and more men and women believed in the Lord and were added to their number. [15] As a result, people brought the sick into the streets and laid them on beds and mats so that at least Peter's shadow might fall on some of them as he passed by. [16] Crowds gathered also from the towns around Jerusalem, bringing their sick and those tormented by evil spirits, and all of them were healed.

B. Persecution Arises

Acts 5:40-42

[40] They called the apostles in and had them flogged. Then they ordered them not to speak in the name of Jesus, and let them go. [41] The apostles left the Sanhedrin, rejoicing because they had been counted worthy of suffering disgrace for the Name. [42] Day after day, in the temple courts and from house to house, they never stopped teaching and proclaiming the good news that Jesus is the Christ.

Acts 8:1

And Saul was there, giving approval to his [Stephen's] death. On that day a great persecution broke out against the church at Jerusalem, and all except the apostles were scattered throughout Judea and Samaria.

C. Jesus-Story Moves beyond Jerusalem

A MIGHTY SOURCE

JESUS' LIFE

ONE IMPORTANT ASPECT OF ANY STORY IS ITS SETTING. IT GIVES A STORY CONTEXT.

THE SAME IS TRUE IN UNDERSTANDING JESUS' LIFE.

JESUS WAS BORN IN BETHLEHEM BUT GREW UP IN NAZARETH. HIS FATHER WAS A STONEWORKER

JESUS' FIRST CHAIR

BORING

Cafe

DIED IN JERUSALEM RESURRECTED IN

MIRACLE IN BETHSAIDA

CALLED DISCIPLES IN CAPERNAUM

LIVED IN NAZARETH

BORN IN BETHLEHEM

JESUS STARTED HIS MINISTRY IN CAPERNAUM WHERE HE CHOSE DISCIPLES

THE MAIN INDUSTRY WAS FISHING

FISHING FOR MEN? WE'RE GONNA NEED A BIGGER NET.

JES

THE CHURCH

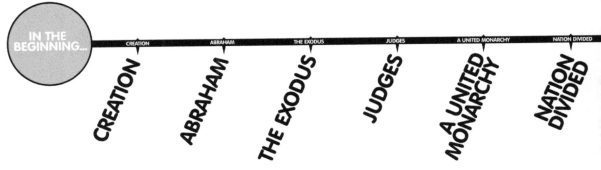

IN THE BEGINNING...

CREATION

ABRAHAM

THE EXODUS

JUDGES

A UNITED MONARCHY

NATION DIVIDED

CREATION

ABRAHAM

THE EXODUS

JUDGES

A UNITED MONARCHY

NATION DIVIDED

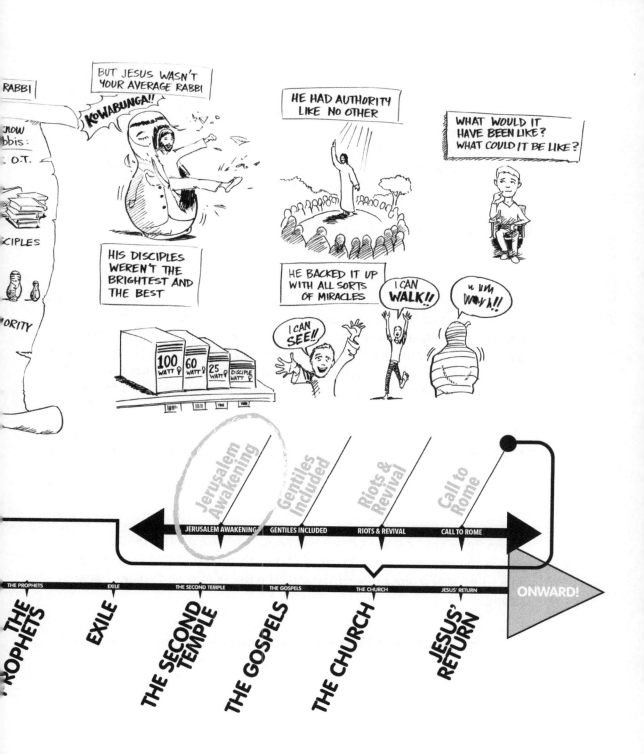

DISCUSSION

Using the questions that follow, we will review and expand on the teaching we just experienced.

Luke 19:41-44

41 As he approached Jerusalem and saw the city, he wept over it 42 and said, "If you, even you, had only known on this day what would bring you peace—but now it is hidden from your eyes. 43 The days will come upon you when your enemies will build an embankment against you and encircle you and hem you in on every side. 44 They will dash you to the ground, you and the children within your walls. They will not leave one stone on another, because you did not recognize the time of God's coming to you."

1 Why did Jesus weep over Jerusalem?

Acts 2:1-4

1 When the day of Pentecost came, they were all together in one place. 2 Suddenly a sound like the blowing of a violent wind came from heaven and filled the whole house where they were sitting. 3 They saw what seemed to be tongues of fire that separated and came to rest on each of them. 4 All of them were filled with the Holy Spirit and began to speak in other tongues as the Spirit enabled them.

2 What event signaled the beginning of the awakening in Jerusalem?

Acts 3:6-7

6 Then Peter said, "Silver or gold I do not have, but what I do have I give you. In the name of Jesus Christ of Nazareth, walk." 7 Taking him by the right hand, he helped him up, and instantly the man's feet and ankles became strong.

3 Which miracles caused Peter and John to be arrested and interrogated?

Acts 5:14-16

¹⁴ Nevertheless, more and more men and women believed in the Lord and were added to their number. ¹⁵ As a result, people brought the sick into the streets and laid them on beds and mats so that at least Peter's shadow might fall on some of them as he passed by. ¹⁶ Crowds gathered also from the towns around Jerusalem, bringing their sick and those tormented by impure spirits, and all of them were healed.

4 For what purpose did the crowds gather from the surrounding towns and villages?

Acts 8:1

And Saul was there, giving approval to his [Stephen's] death. On that day a great persecution broke out against the church in Jerusalem, and all except the apostles were scattered throughout Judea and Samaria.

5 What was the result of the persecution persecution of the

Jerusalem church?

APPLICATION

Now it's time to make some personal applications of all we've been thinking about in the last few minutes.

READ ALOUD

The people of Jerusalem failed to recognize the opportunity before them when Jesus was in the city. They were distracted by other messages and too busy with their own agendas. However, after Jesus' ascension, another opportunity was extended to the inhabitants of Jerusalem. On the Day of Pentecost, the Holy Spirit was poured out and the disciples were changed. The outcome was a series of events that awakened the city to the reality of a living Jesus.

> John 14:12
>
> *"I tell you the truth, anyone who has faith in me will do what I have been doing. He will do even greater things than these, because I am going to the Father."*

6 In Acts 2:1-4, Jerusalem is awakened to a living Jesus. In what ways does Peter's ministry attest to "even greater things" than Jesus had done during His days in Jerusalem?

7 How do you think the disciples felt after they failed to stand up for Jesus when He was arrested and suffered?

8 How would the previous experience have impacted them when they had another opportunity in the same city?

Acts 4:29-30

²⁹ "Now, Lord, consider their threats and enable your servants to speak your word with great boldness. ³⁰ Stretch out your hand to heal and perform miraculous signs and wonders through the name of your holy servant Jesus."

9 Even after being arrested and threatened, what were the disciples asking God to do?

10 Describe a time you failed to "stand up for Jesus" when you had an opportunity.

41

READ ALOUD

Failure is not final. We all have failed in our faithfulness and our faith. We are not failures. God forgives and is able to restore. He will even provide future opportunities to honor Him. We have the assignment of being prepared. The Day of Pentecost was a part of the disciples' preparation. God's involvement with them opened doors for them to tell their story. The same is true today.

11 What role does the Holy Spirit occupy in your spiritual life?

12 How has your awareness of the Holy Spirit changed in the last year?

READ ALOUD

In the midst of awakening, the disciples experienced remarkable miracles. There were healings, people were delivered, large groups of people were responding to the messages—the city was stirred. There was also aggressive resistance and persecution. Often we fail to imagine that resistance accompanies awakening. If we are not prepared, we may forfeit our opportunity.

13 In what ways is the Jesus-message resisted in our communities?

14 God's supernatural involvement opened doors of opportunity; it still does. Discuss answers to prayer, miracles you have experienced, and the opportunities presented.

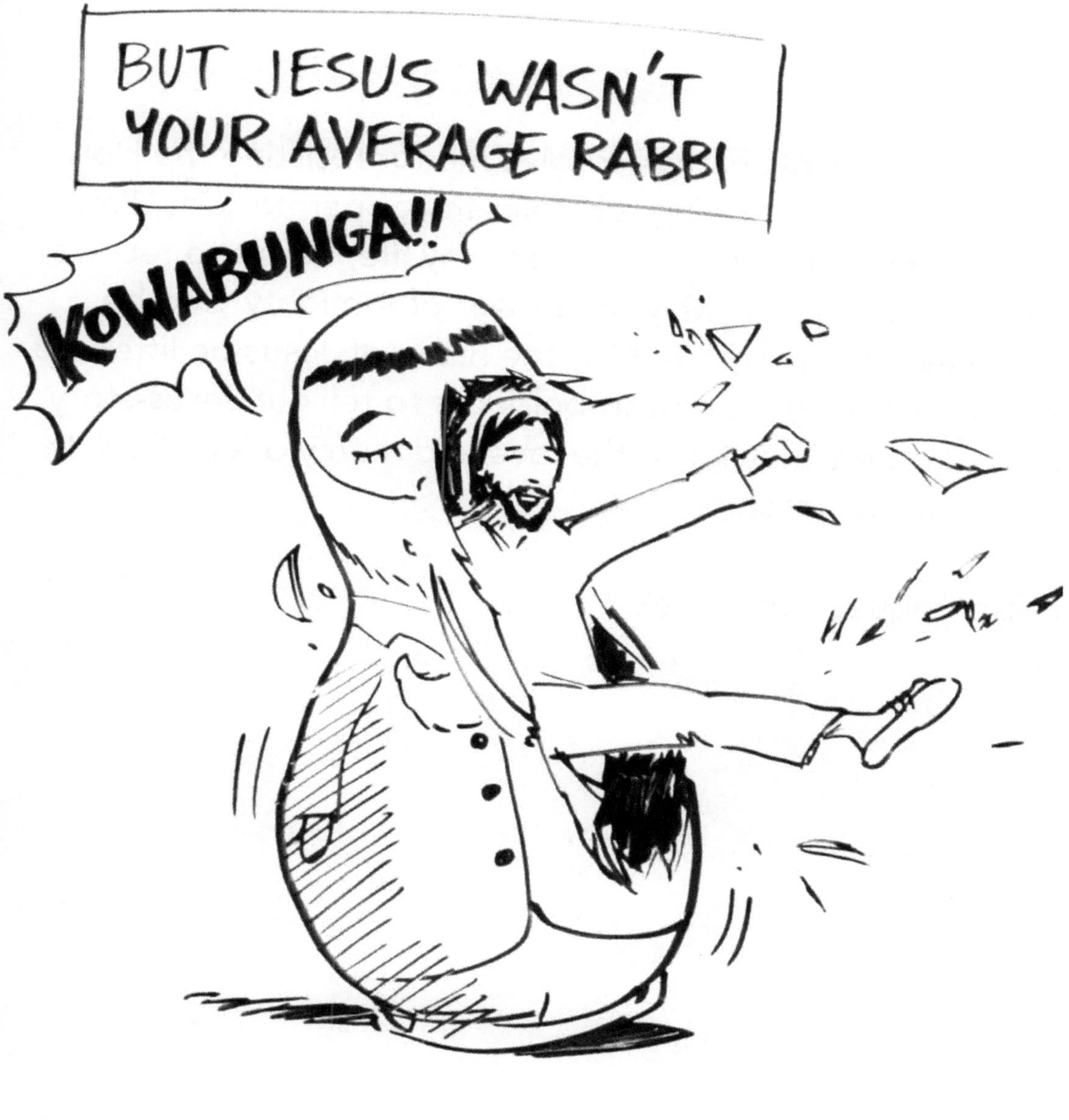
BUT JESUS WASN'T YOUR AVERAGE RABBI
KOWABUNGA!!

PRAYER

Close the session in prayer. Share prayer requests with the group, and pray for each other. Close by praying the following prayer together.

Heavenly Father, forgive me for resisting the Holy Spirit, for being reluctant to cooperate with Him. Pour out Your Spirit upon my life; I want to receive all You have for me. May the power of Almighty God be made evident in my life. May the name of Jesus be lifted up in our community. Grant us boldness to tell our Jesus-story so that others may know the love and mercy of our God. In Jesus' name, amen.

Prayer requests this week:

GOING DEEPER

This section is designed to do as homework, if you choose, between your Small Group meetings.

Acts 5:27-42

27 Having brought the apostles, they made them appear before the Sanhedrin to be questioned by the high priest. 28 "We gave you strict orders not to teach in this name," he said. "Yet you have filled Jerusalem with your teaching and are determined to make us guilty of this man's blood." 29 Peter and the other apostles replied: "We must obey God rather than men! 30 The God of our fathers raised Jesus from the dead—whom you had killed by hanging him on a tree. 31 God exalted him to his own right hand as Prince and Savior that he might give repentance and forgiveness of sins to Israel. 32 We are witnesses of these things, and so is the Holy Spirit, whom God has given to those who obey him." 33 When they heard this, they were furious and wanted to put them to death. 34 But a Pharisee named Gamaliel, a teacher of the law, who was honored by all the people, stood up in the Sanhedrin and ordered that the men be put outside for a little while. 35 Then he addressed them: "Men of Israel, consider carefully what you intend to do to these men. 36 Some time ago Theudas appeared, claiming to be somebody, and about four hundred men rallied to him. He was killed, all his followers were dispersed, and it all came to nothing. 37 After him, Judas the Galilean appeared in the days of the census and led a band of people in revolt. He too was killed, and all his followers were scattered. 38 Therefore, in the present case I advise you: Leave these men alone! Let them go! For if their purpose or activity is of human origin, it will fail. 39 But if it is from God, you will not be able to stop these men; you will only find yourselves fighting against God." 40 His speech persuaded them. They called the apostles in and had them flogged. Then they ordered them not to speak in the name of Jesus, and let them go. 41 The apostles left the Sanhedrin, rejoicing because they had been counted worthy of suffering disgrace for the Name. 42 Day after day, in the temple courts and from house to house, they never stopped teaching and proclaiming the good news that Jesus is the Christ.

In the midst of persecution and threats, the disciples would not yield. They persisted under pressure and cooperated with the Holy Spirit, which resulted in awakening spreading through Jerusalem and the surrounding areas. They witnessed under the threat of not just being disliked but losing their lives. We often have pushback against our faith. We cannot let our faith be diminished because of the intensity of the challenges in our lives. Just as with the disciples, He will use your God-story for His purposes. The awakening Jesus puts in you is not only for you but for all those you influence. Pressure and persecution toward the disciples produced great joy, multiplication, and miracles.

- Read vv. 28-30. What were the orders of the Sanhedrin to the disciples? What was the motivation behind their threat?

- How did Peter and the other apostles respond?

- Jesus prepared His disciples by giving them boldness through the Holy Spirit to stand in the midst of great pressure. Can you remember a time the Holy Spirit helped you take a stand for your faith? What was the outcome?

- What fears have you faced when making decisions to say yes to God? How have you overcome those fears?

- Sharing your God-story takes intentionality. Do you have someone in your influence with whom you have not shared your faith? When you are willing, ask the Holy Spirit to open the door for you to speak to this person.

DAILY REFLECTIONS

These are daily reviews of the key Bible verses and related others that will help you think about and apply the insights from this session.

DAY 1

Luke 18:27

Only God

Jesus replied, "What is impossible with men is possible with God."

Reflection Question:
How does this verse challenge a believer to take an even greater risk when dealing with spiritual things?

DAY 2

Acts 1:6-7

Instructions

⁶ So when they met together, they asked him, "Lord, are you at this time going to restore the kingdom to Israel?" ⁷ He said to them: "It is not for you to know the times or dates the Father has set by his own authority."

Reflection Question:
Do you have any prayers from your list that appear to be out of God's view? Are you looking at the wrong things for this season?

DAY 3

John 16:12-13

Truth

¹² "I have much more to say to you, more than you can now bear. ¹³ But when he, the Spirit of truth, comes, he will guide you into all truth. He will not speak on his own; he will speak only what he hears, and he will tell you what is yet to come."

Reflection Question:
How helpful was the promise of the Holy Spirit in the lives of the disciples in the Jerusalem awakening? How do we need His help in the Church today? Can you think of a few places in your life where you need the Spirit of Truth?

DAY 4

Acts 5:42

Persevere

Day after day, in the temple courts and from house to house, they never stopped teaching and proclaiming the good news that Jesus is the Christ.

Reflection Question:
Do you ever get tired of acting like a Christ-follower? At church and in our homes we have endless opportunities to obey Him. Ask God to refresh your list of ways to serve and obey Him.

_____

_____

_____

_____

_____

DAY 5

Acts 3:19-20

Refreshing

¹⁹ Repent, then, and turn to God, so that your sins may be wiped out, that times of refreshing may come from the Lord, ²⁰ and that he may send the Christ, who has been appointed for you—even Jesus.

Reflection Question:
How do you need refreshing today?

_____

_____

_____

_____

_____

WEEKLY MEMORY VERSE

WEEK 3

INTRODUCTION

The Church is a supernatural initiative. It has survived and flourished for two millennia. Empires have come and gone, but the Church continues forward. Jesus is the head of the Church; through His faithfulness and obedience the Church was brought forth. He will watch over the completion of the story. Our lesson this week focuses on a seismic shift in the direction of the Church. The non-Jewish world is going to be invited to participate—on equal footing. This type of a change required supernatural intervention to initiate.

GENTILES INCLUDED

It is important to remember that Jesus is still watching over His Church. The greatest honor extended to a human being is the privilege of participating with Almighty God in His purposes in the earth. Christ-followers are far more than people who attend worship services or persons with a moral code—we are children of the King. The Church is the expression of God's love and truth to the world.

THE CHURCH

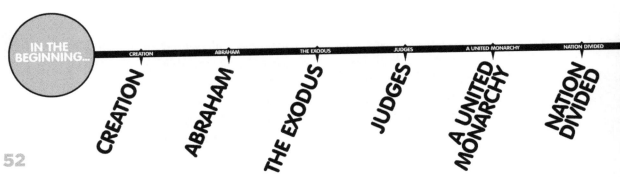

IN THE BEGINNING...

CREATION

ABRAHAM

THE EXODUS

JUDGES

A UNITED MONARCHY

NATION DIVIDED

CREATION

ABRAHAM

THE EXODUS

JUDGES

A UNITED MONARCHY

NATION DIVIDED

52

GETTING STARTED

Begin the session with a question below or brief activity to become better acquainted with one another.

1 Describe a time you changed your mind about something you believe about God.

2 Share something that surprised you as you read your Bible.

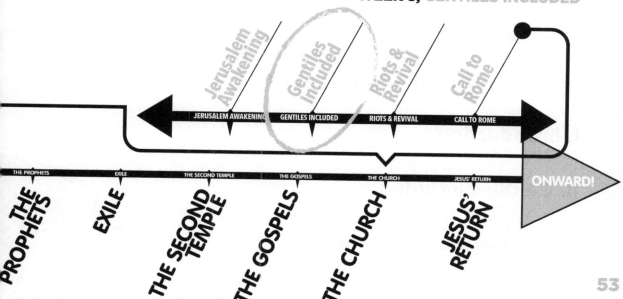

JERUSALEM AWAKENING   GENTILES INCLUDED   RIOTS & REVIVAL   CALL TO ROME

Jerusalem Awakening

Gentiles Included

Riots & Revival

Call to Rome

THE PROPHETS   EXILE   THE SECOND TEMPLE   THE GOSPELS   THE CHURCH   JESUS' RETURN

THE PROPHETS

EXILE

THE SECOND TEMPLE

THE GOSPELS

THE CHURCH

JESUS' RETURN

ONWARD!

LUKE WROTE HIS JESUS STORY IN TWO PARTS:

GOSPEL of LUKE

BOOK OF ACTS *THE SEQUEL*

OUTLINE OF DVD LESSON

Use the outline below to follow along during the DVD.

I. Introduction

II. Gentiles Included

A. Jesus Recruits Saul of Tarsus

Acts 9:1-6

¹ Meanwhile, Saul was still breathing out murderous threats against the Lord's disciples. He went to the high priest ² and asked him for letters to the synagogues in Damascus, so that if he found any there who belonged to the Way, whether men or women, he might take them as prisoners to Jerusalem. ³ As he neared Damascus on his journey, suddenly a light from heaven flashed around him. ⁴ He fell to the ground and heard a voice say to him, "Saul, Saul, why do you persecute me?" ⁵ "Who are you, Lord?" Saul asked. "I am Jesus, whom you are persecuting," he replied. ⁶ "Now get up and go into the city, and you will be told what you must do."

Philippians 3:4-6

⁴ If anyone else thinks he has reasons to put confidence in the flesh, I have more: ⁵ circumcised on the eighth day, of the people of Israel, of the tribe of Benjamin, a Hebrew of Hebrews; in regard to the law, a Pharisee; ⁶ as for zeal, persecuting the church; as for legalistic righteousness, faultless.

B. Peter Sent to a Roman Centurion

Acts 10:9-15

⁹ About noon the following day as they were on their journey and approaching the city, Peter went up on the roof to pray. ¹⁰ He became hungry and wanted something to eat, and while the meal was being prepared, he fell into a trance. ¹¹ He saw heaven opened and something like a large sheet being let down to earth by its four corners. ¹² It contained all kinds of four-footed animals, as well as reptiles of the earth and birds of the air. ¹³ Then a voice told him, "Get up, Peter. Kill and eat." ¹⁴ "Surely not, Lord!" Peter replied. "I have never eaten anything impure or unclean."

¹⁵ *The voice spoke to him a second time, "Do not call anything impure that God has made clean."*

1. Peter travels to Caesarea
Acts 10:34-38

³⁴ *Then Peter began to speak: "I now realize how true it is that God does not show favoritism* ³⁵ *but accepts men from every nation who fear him and do what is right.* ³⁶ *You know the message God sent to the people of Israel, telling the good news of peace through Jesus Christ, who is Lord of all.* ³⁷ *You know what has happened throughout Judea, beginning in Galilee after the baptism that John preached—* ³⁸ *how God anointed Jesus of Nazareth with the Holy Spirit and power, and how he went around doing good and healing all who were under the power of the devil, because God was with him."*

2. Events of Pentecost in Jerusalem are repeated
Acts 10:44-46

⁴⁴ *While Peter was still speaking these words, the Holy Spirit came on all who heard the message.* ⁴⁵ *The circumcised believers who had come with Peter were astonished that the gift of the Holy Spirit had been poured out even on the Gentiles.* ⁴⁶ *For they heard them speaking in tongues and praising God.*

C. Observations

1. God accepts people from every nation.
2. Jesus is Lord of ALL.
3. The Holy Spirit descends on Cornelius and his friends.
4. The Jewish believers are astonished.

D. No One Is Left Out—the Jesus-Story Is Open for All

A MIGHTY SOURCE
ASCENSION & EARLY CHURCH
LAST WEEK:

JESUS

JESUS CHANGES LIVES

HOW DID THEY CHANGE?

LUKE WROTE HIS JESUS STORY IN TWO PARTS:

GOSPEL of LUKE

BOOK OF ACTS THE SEQUEL

AFTER JESUS CAME BACK TO LIFE HE HAD SOME FINAL INSTRUCTIONS.

AND THEN HE LEFT THEM.

GO & TELL

WHOA

THE BOOK OF ACTS SAYS HIS FOLLOWERS LISTENED & ACTED

THEY FIRST CHANGED BY SHARING ALL THEY HAD

AND THEY INVITED OTHERS TO THIS WAY OF LIFE

SE WHA MIN IS YOUR

SO THERE IT IS

WHO WANTS TO JOIN?

WE'RE GONNA NEED MORE WELCOME PACKS

THOUSANDS AT A TIM

THE CHURCH

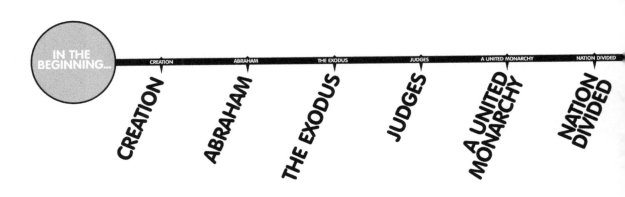

IN THE BEGINNING...

CREATION

ABRAHAM

THE EXODUS

JUDGES

A UNITED MONARCHY

NATION DIVIDED

CREATION

ABRAHAM

THE EXODUS

JUDGES

A UNITED MONARCHY

NATION DIVIDED

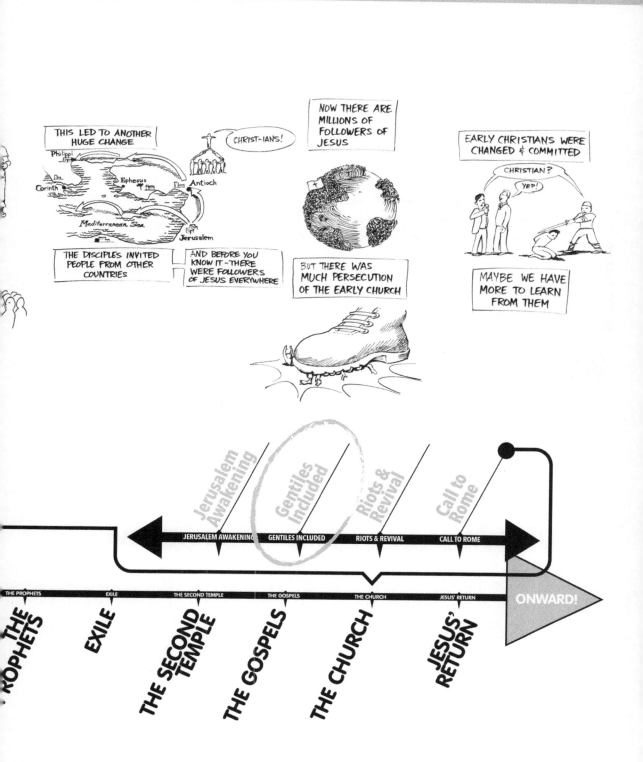

DISCUSSION

Using the questions that follow, we will review and expand on the teaching we just experienced.

1 Describe Saul's attitude and ambitions when we are first introduced to him.

Galatians 1:13-18

13 For you have heard of my previous way of life in Judaism, how intensely I persecuted the church of God and tried to destroy it. 14 I was advancing in Judaism beyond many Jews of my own age and was extremely zealous for the traditions of my fathers. 15 But when God, who set me apart from birth and called me by his grace, was pleased 16 to reveal his Son in me so that I might preach him among the Gentiles, I did not consult any man, 17 nor did I go up to Jerusalem to see those who were apostles before I was, but I went immediately into Arabia and later returned to Damascus. 18 Then after three years, I went up to Jerusalem to get acquainted with Peter and stayed with him fifteen days.

2 In these verses, how does Paul describe his attitude toward the Church?

3 How many years did Paul prepare before he went to meet Peter?

4 What initiated Peter's visit to Caesarea?

5 Why was Cornelius, a Roman centurion, willing to listen to Peter, a Jewish fisherman?

6 In Cornelius's home, who was most surprised by the events that unfolded?

APPLICATION

Now it's time to make some personal applications of all we've been thinking about in the last few minutes.

READ ALOUD

In Acts 9 and 10, the direction of the emerging Church took a dramatic turn. Up until this point, the Church had been almost entirely Jewish. Two things happened to change this: Jesus personally recruited a zealous rabbi for his cause, and Peter participated in Pentecost 2—this time in a non-Jewish community. The Jesus-story was going global.

Acts 9:1-6

1 Meanwhile, Saul was still breathing out murderous threats against the Lord's disciples. He went to the high priest 2 and asked him for letters to the synagogues in Damascus, so that if he found any there who belonged to the Way, whether men or women, he might take them as prisoners to Jerusalem. 3 As he neared Damascus on his journey, suddenly a light from heaven flashed around him. 4 He fell to the ground and heard a voice say to him, "Saul, Saul, why do you persecute me?" 5 "Who are you, Lord?" Saul asked. "I am Jesus, whom you are persecuting," he replied. 6 "Now get up and go into the city, and you will be told what you must do."

7 Jesus issued new orders to Saul. Describe a time Jesus redirected your life.

READ ALOUD

Jesus, in dramatic fashion, established His authority in Saul's life. Yielding to this authority brought radical changes to Saul's life—new career, new friends, new ways of understanding the world. Certainly, many who had known Saul prior to his Jesus-encounter were frustrated and concerned about his change. Saul had encountered a greater power. Authority is the exercise of power. When we reject God's authority to provide direction, we forfeit the benefit of His power.

8 List some of the ways God's power was made apparent in Saul's life. Read Acts 16:16-18; Acts 16:25-26; and Acts 19:11-12.

9 Yielding to God's authority opens our lives to His power. Describe a time you struggled to yield to God's authority. What were the benefits that resulted from cooperation?

READ ALOUD

In the following passage, God redirects Peter's focus. He directs him toward people who Peter would have rejected. Often we imagine God needs to redirect the pagans. Typically God redirects His people to be more effective in helping the unbelievers understand Him. We must be willing to change and grow for the purposes of God to expand. The assignment is not to rage against the darkness but to allow God to brighten His light through us.

61

THE WHITEBOARD BIBLE

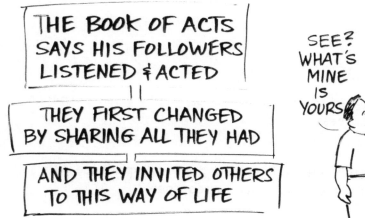

Acts 10:9-15

⁹ About noon the following day as they were on their journey and approaching the city, Peter went up on the roof to pray. ¹⁰ He became hungry and wanted something to eat, and while the meal was being prepared, he fell into a trance. ¹¹ He saw heaven opened and something like a large sheet being let down to earth by its four corners. ¹² It contained all kinds of four-footed animals, as well as reptiles of the earth and birds of the air. ¹³ Then a voice told him, "Get up, Peter. Kill and eat." ¹⁴ "Surely not, Lord!" Peter replied. "I have never eaten anything impure or unclean." ¹⁵ The voice spoke to him a second time, "Do not call anything impure that God has made clean."

Acts 10:34-36

³⁴ Then Peter began to speak: "I now realize how true it is that God does not show favoritism ³⁵ but accepts men from every nation who fear him and do what is right. ³⁶ You know the message God sent to the people of Israel, telling the good news of peace through Jesus Christ, who is Lord of all."

10 What does Peter realize?

11 Which of the following may have been hard for you to process: new styles of music at church, casual dress of attenders, casual dress of minister, changes in service day/time, serving coffee at church, people raising their hands, larger churches?

2 Corinthians 5:21

God made him who had no sin to be sin for us, so that in him we might become the righteousness of God.

12 It is easy to confuse personal preference or previous experience with righteousness. What is the basis of our righteousness?

READ ALOUD

We yield to Jesus' authority and His power begins to change us. Often we imagine the necessity of God's power to change others or our circumstances. Typically God begins with a change within us. We humble ourselves and yield to His authority, and then we see the expressions of His power. After Paul and Peter yielded to God, the world opened up to the Jesus-story. The books of the New Testament are written to believers in Gentile cities, not the cities of Israel. Prior to Acts 9 and 10, we would have expected the letters to be written to Capernaum, Bethlehem, or Nazareth.

13 Pray for one another in areas where you struggle to yield. Simple explanations are sufficient.

63

THE **WHITEBOARD** BIBLE

PRAYER

Close the session in prayer. Share prayer requests with the group, and pray for each other. Close by praying the following prayer together.

Heavenly Father, we rejoice in Your great love for us. You are a God who forgives and redeems. I come in humility to acknowledge my need for a savior. Through the blood of Jesus, all my sins are forgiven. Through the blood of Jesus, I am redeemed out of the hand of the devil. Through the blood of Jesus, I am sanctified, made holy, set apart to God. I rejoice in Your total provision for my life. In Jesus' name, amen.

Prayer requests this week:

GOING DEEPER

This section is designed to do as homework, if you choose, between your Small Group meetings.

Acts 10:30-33

30 Cornelius answered: "Four days ago I was in my house praying at this hour, at three in the afternoon. Suddenly a man in shining clothes stood before me 31 and said, 'Cornelius, God has heard your prayer and remembered your gifts to the poor. 32 Send to Joppa for Simon who is called Peter. He is a guest in the home of Simon the tanner, who lives by the sea.' 33 So I sent for you immediately, and it was good of you to come. Now we are all here in the presence of God to listen to everything the Lord has commanded you to tell us."

Acts 10:44-48

44 While Peter was still speaking these words, the Holy Spirit came on all who heard the message. 45 The circumcised believers who had come with Peter were astonished that the gift of the Holy Spirit had been poured out even on the Gentiles. 46 For they heard them speaking in tongues and praising God. Then Peter said, 47 "Can anyone keep these people from being baptized with water? They have received the Holy Spirit just as we have." 48 So he ordered that they be baptized in the name of Jesus Christ. Then they asked Peter to stay with them for a few days.

Peter, a devout Jew, was prohibited from associating with Gentiles. Yet he is called to Caesarea, a pagan city, to bring the news of Jesus to Cornelius and his household. God's supernatural intervention made it possible for the barrier to be broken. The message God gave is that the Jesus-story is open for all. God is a restorer and redeemer to those who yield to Him. He gives us meaningful places in His purposes when we cooperate with Him.

- Read vv. 30-31. Who paid a visit to Cornelius? Why was Cornelius chosen for the visitation?

- Faithful prayer, willingness to give, and the fear of the Lord put Cornelius and his whole family on God's radar. Which area of your life would you like to transform this year?

- In the Jewish law it was forbidden that you should associate with Gentiles. God gave Peter a vision that resulted in Gentiles hearing the good news of Jesus. Has there been a time in your life when you felt as though you were on the outside of God's reach or somehow disqualified?

- An awakening to the reality that God loves us so much that there are absolutely no barriers to our potential in Him is vital to fulfilling His purpose for us. Take a moment and ask God to help you overcome any imagined limitations.

- Read v. 33. What was Cornelius's attitude when Peter arrived? How would you rate yourself on the expectation of God speaking to you? Do you come to church ready to hear a message that you can apply to your life? Pray about how you may prepare your heart to receive God's message for you.

- Read vv. 44-48. Who were the recipients of the baptism in the Holy Spirit? What was the reaction of the circumcised believers?

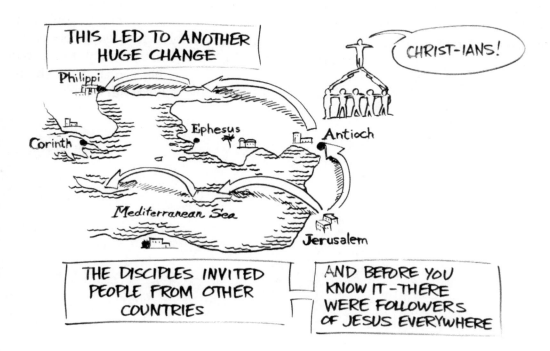

DAILY REFLECTIONS

These are daily reviews of the key Bible verses and related others that will help you think about and apply the insights from this session.

DAY 1

Acts 6:7

God's Word

So the Word of God spread. The number of disciples in Jerusalem increased rapidly, and a large number of priests became obedient to the faith.

Reflection Question:
Why do you think the Word of God spread? What would happen in your community, your neighborhood, or your family if the Word of God is given out in more ways?

DAY 2

Acts 10:34-35

Good News

³⁴ Then Peter began to speak: "I now realize how true it is that God does not show favoritism ³⁵ but accepts men from every nation who fear him and do what is right."

Reflection Question:
Think about the gift we have received, knowing that God doesn't favor one person above another when He deals with us. Are you a person who fears God and does what is right?

DAY 3

Acts 3:6-7

Help for Healing

⁶ Then Peter said, "Silver or gold I do not have, but what I have I give you. In the name of Jesus Christ of Nazareth, walk." ⁷ Taking him by the right hand, he helped him up, and instantly the man's feet and ankles became strong.

Reflection Question:
What is your most valuable resource? What has God given you to share with the people around you? Can you see people become strong enough to stand on their own after you share Christ with them?

DAY 4

Acts 2:42-43

Fellowship

⁴² *They devoted themselves to the apostles' teaching and to the fellowship, to the breaking of bread and to prayer.* ⁴³ *Everyone was filled with awe at the many wonders and signs performed by the apostles.*

Reflection Question:
How can you prepare to receive from God?

_____

_____

_____

_____

_____

_____

DAY 5

Acts 4:12

No Other Name

"Salvation is found in no one else, for there is no other name under heaven given to men by which we must be saved."

Reflection Question:
This verse clarifies that there are not "many roads to God." The Lord has given us truth to keep us from straying away from His Word. Is the name of Jesus honored by your life? Reflect for a moment for any area that would benefit from repentance.

_____

_____

_____

_____

_____

WEEKLY MEMORY VERSE

"SALVATION IS FOUND IN NO ONE ELSE, FOR THERE IS NO OTHER NAME UNDER HEAVEN GIVEN TO MEN BY WHICH WE MUST BE SAVED."

ACTS 4:12

WEEK 4

INTRODUCTION

In so many ways the Bible is a surprising book. When a woman asked Jesus for help and He initially refused her because she was not Jewish, it seems to be a startling response. A man in a synagogue was healed, and the reaction of the leaders was anger, not joy. These unexpected responses continue throughout the New Testament. The Church gained momentum and began to spread beyond Jerusalem and then beyond Israel. The faithfulness of the messengers was combined with the miraculous involvement

RIOTS and REVIVAL

of God. What is surprising is the bitterness of the opposition. Often, but not always, it emerged from the religious community. One thing is consistent; the Jesus-story did not go forward without very real and very physical challenges.

There is nothing in the Bible to suggest that the pattern would change in the twenty-first century. God still uses faithful messengers and confirms His Word supernaturally. Opposition to the Jesus-story persists. The Jesus-initiative moves forward with men and women who demonstrate courage in telling their story. The Church today is an extension of the churches in Jerusalem, Corinth, Ephesus, Rome, and the others that fill the New Testament.

THE CHURCH

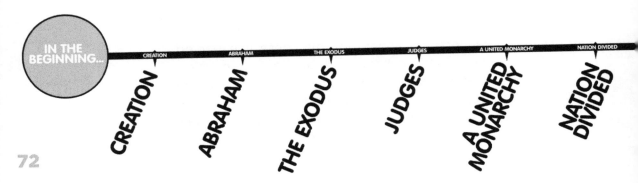

IN THE BEGINNING...

CREATION

ABRAHAM

THE EXODUS

JUDGES

A UNITED MONARCHY

NATION DIVIDED

CREATION

ABRAHAM

THE EXODUS

JUDGES

A UNITED MONARCHY

NATION DIVIDED

72

GETTING STARTED

Begin the session with a question below or brief activity to become better acquainted with one another.

1 Describe the most problematic trip you have ever taken.

2 Where would you most like to visit and why?

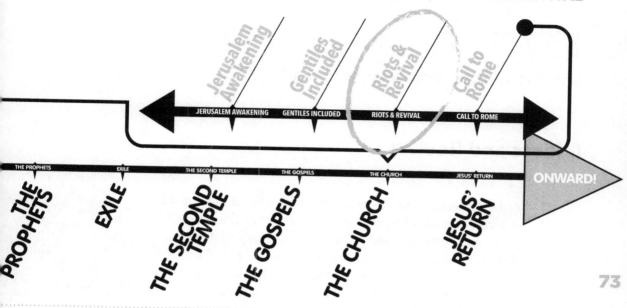

OUTLINE OF DVD LESSON

Use the outline below to follow along during the DVD.

I. Riots and Revival

Acts 11:19-21

19 Now those who had been scattered by the persecution in connection with Stephen traveled as far as Phoenicia, Cyprus and Antioch, telling the message only to Jews. 20 Some of them, however, men from Cyprus and Cyrene, went to Antioch and began to speak to Greeks also, telling them the good news about the Lord Jesus. 21 The Lord's hand was with them, and a great number of people believed and turned to the Lord.

A. Pattern for the Expanding Church

Acts 13:49-52

49 The word of the Lord spread through the whole region. 50 But the Jews incited the God-fearing women of high standing and the leading men of the city. They stirred up persecution against Paul and Barnabas, and expelled them from their region. 51 So they shook the dust from their feet in protest against them and went to Iconium. 52 And the disciples were filled with joy and with the Holy Spirit.

B. Communities of Faith That Fill Our New Testament

1. Ephesus
2. Athens
3. Corinth
4. Thessalonica
5. Galatia
6. Rome

C. Paul Endured Much
2 Corinthians 11:23-28

²³ I have worked much harder, been in prison more frequently, been flogged more severely, and been exposed to death again and again. ²⁴ Five times I received from the Jews the forty lashes minus one. ²⁵ Three times I was beaten with rods, once I was stoned, three times I was shipwrecked, I spent a night and a day in the open sea, ²⁶ I have been constantly on the move. I have been in danger from rivers, in danger from bandits, in danger from my own countrymen, in danger from Gentiles; in danger in the city, in danger in the country, in danger at sea; and in danger from false brothers. ²⁷ I have labored and toiled and have often gone without sleep; I have known hunger and thirst and have often gone without food; I have been cold and naked. ²⁸ Besides everything else, I face daily the pressure of my concern for all the churches."

D. Acts Reminds Us of the Larger Story of Scripture

1. God, a plan for His people
2. Jesus, God's ultimate provision for humanity

E. Our Response

1. Jesus as Christ and Lord
2. Repentance
3. Baptism
4. Holy Spirit—in the midst of the Church
5. Life redirected

Philippians 3:12

Not that I have already obtained all this, or have already been made perfect, but I press on to take hold of that for which Christ Jesus took hold of me.

THE CHURCH

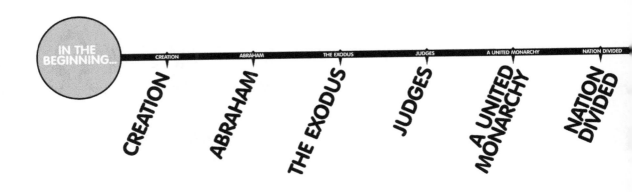

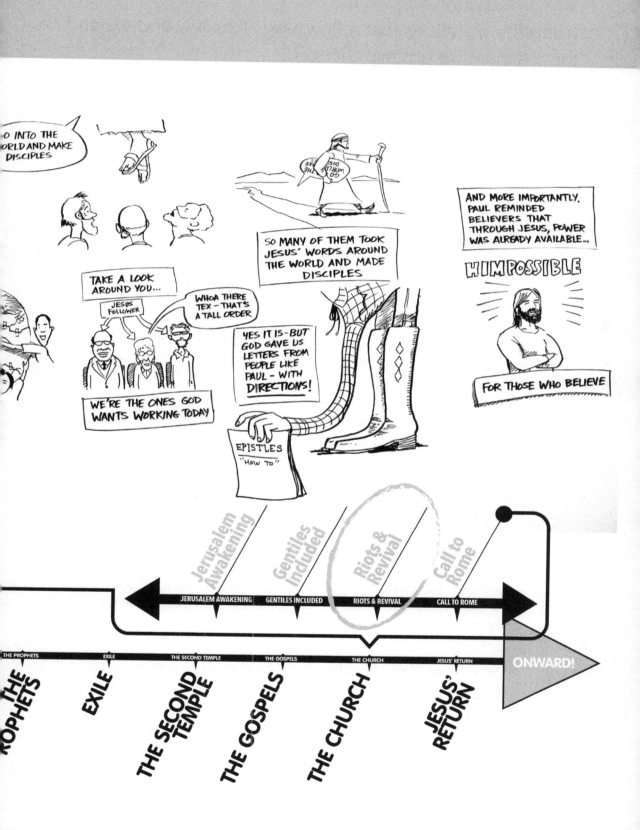

DISCUSSION

Using the questions that follow, we will review and expand on the teaching we just experienced.

Acts 11:19-21

[19] *Now those who had been scattered by the persecution in connection with Stephen traveled as far as Phoenicia, Cyprus and Antioch, telling the message only to Jews.* [20] *Some of them, however, men from Cyprus and Cyrene, went to Antioch and began to speak to Greeks also, telling them the good news about the Lord Jesus.* [21] *The Lord's hand was with them, and a great number of people believed and turned to the Lord.*

1 What launched the Church into Phoenicia, Cyprus, and Antioch?

2 Why do you think the disciples had such an urgency to tell their story? On a scale of 1-10, evaluate the urgency you feel to tell your Jesus-story.

3 In your opinion, what gave the early disciples such courage?

Acts 19:23-26

[23] *About that time there arose a great disturbance about the Way.* [24] *A silversmith named Demetrius, who made silver shrines of Artemis, brought in no little business for the craftsmen.* [25] *He called them together, along with the workmen in related trades, and said: "Men, you know we receive a good income from this business.* [26] *And you see and hear how this fellow Paul has convinced and led astray large numbers of people here in Ephesus and in practically the whole province of Asia. He says that man-made gods are no gods at all."*

4 What motivated the opposition to Paul and his team in Ephesus?

GOD ALSO MADE IT
CLEAR THAT ANYONE
CAN FOLLOW HIM

AND CONTRIBUTE
TO FIXING A
BROKEN WORLD

APPLICATION

Now it's time to make some personal applications of all we've been thinking about in the last few minutes.

READ ALOUD

The early disciples experienced remarkable things as they shared their Jesus-stories. People responded in great numbers, God responded with remarkable miracles, and they expanded the scope of their ministries. They were anything but static. There is no suggestion that serving Jesus consisted of a quiet meeting for a few minutes each week. Let's revisit Acts 11 and consider the implications for our lives.

Acts 11:19-21

19 Now those who had been scattered by the persecution in connection with Stephen traveled as far as Phoenicia, Cyprus and Antioch, telling the message only to Jews. 20 Some of them, however, men from Cyprus and Cyrene, went to Antioch and began to speak to Greeks also, telling them the good news about the Lord Jesus. 21 The Lord's hand was with them, and a great number of people believed and turned to the Lord.

5 Scattered is an agricultural word. In reality, the disciples were driven from their homes and communities because of their living faith. In verse 21, we are told "the Lord's hand was with them." How do you reconcile God's being with them and their being "scattered"?

6 Describe ways the American Church faces opposition. How has this impacted your experience and choices?

7   How do you combat the temptation to be a "private Christ-follower"?

8   Where is it most difficult for you to discuss your faith? Where do you find it the easiest?

READ ALOUD

We often hear people assert a desire to be like the New Testament Church. Such statements usually refer to doctrinal correctness or God's supernatural involvement. It is impossible to consider the early believers without understanding the cost of discipleship. Being a Christ-follower is not simply about having our prayers answered and our needs meet. We are asked to persevere, to endure. The assignment is to continue to live the truth we know even when it would be easier to be ungodly or hide our faith.

THE **WHITEBOARD** BIBLE

9 The Jesus-message is consistently referred to as Good News. Share something good that God has done in your life since you became a Christ-follower.

2 Corinthians 11:23-28

23 *Are they servants of Christ? (I am out of my mind to talk like this.) I am more. I have worked much harder, been in prison more frequently, been flogged more severely, and been exposed to death again and again.* 24 *Five times I received from the Jews the forty lashes minus one.* 25 *Three times I was beaten with rods, once I was stoned, three times I was shipwrecked, I spent a night and a day in the open sea,* 26 *I have been constantly on the move. I have been in danger from rivers, in danger from bandits, in danger from my own countrymen, in danger from Gentiles; in danger in the city, in danger in the country, in danger at sea; and in danger from false brothers.* 27 *I have labored and toiled and have often gone without sleep; I have known hunger and thirst and have often gone without food; I have been cold and naked.* 28 *Besides everything else, I face daily the pressure of my concern for all the churches.*

10 Perseverance is about our willingness to continue. Describe a time when your spiritual life required perseverance.

READ ALOUD

In the previous passage, Paul described more than a dozen physical challenges he had endured as a result of his faith. The outcomes were remarkable but only from the vantage point of history. From the perspective of Paul's traveling companions, he was a bad risk. Even at the end of his life, the churches he had helped to birth were struggling mightily. Read the following passage that was written near the end of his life.

2 Timothy 4:9-18

⁹ Do your best to come to me quickly, ¹⁰ for Demas, because he loved this world, has deserted me and has gone to Thessalonica. Crescens has gone to Galatia, and Titus to Dalmatia. ¹¹ Only Luke is with me. Get Mark and bring him with you, because he is helpful to me in my ministry. ¹² I sent Tychicus to Ephesus. ¹³ When you come, bring the cloak that I left with Carpus at Troas, and my scrolls, especially the parchments. ¹⁴ Alexander the metalworker did me a great deal of harm. The Lord will repay him for what he has done. ¹⁵ You too should be on your guard against him, because he strongly opposed our message. ¹⁶ At my first defense, no one came to my support, but everyone deserted me. May it not be held against them. ¹⁷ But the Lord stood at my side and gave me strength, so that through me the message might be fully proclaimed and all the Gentiles might hear it. And I was delivered from the lion's mouth. ¹⁸ The Lord will rescue me from every evil attack and will bring me safely to his heavenly kingdom. To him be glory for ever and ever. Amen.

11 How would you evaluate Paul's circumstances? Is the personal support and encouragement what you would anticipate?

12 Was the Apostle Paul successful? How does your answer impact your own life goals for success and achievement?

13 Paul was a tentmaker with a message. His message was shaped by his awareness of his great need. He had been a violent, angry man. Our message is shaped by our awareness of God's grace to us. Describe how God's mercy has impacted your spiritual journey.

14 Discuss ways to share your Jesus-story with more boldness in the arenas of influence God has given to you.

PRAYER

Close the session in prayer. Share prayer requests with the group, and pray for each other. Close by praying the following prayer together.

Heavenly Father, thank you for the great gift of Jesus. I rejoice in Your mercy; You have called me out of darkness and welcomed me into the Kingdom of Your Son. Give me boldness to share the good things You have done for me. Open my heart to the opportunities that are before me. Grant me the strength to persevere through all the challenges life presents. May my life bring glory to the name of Jesus. In Jesus' name, amen.

Prayer requests this week:

GOING DEEPER

This section is designed to do as homework, if you choose, between your Small Group meetings.

It seemed wherever Paul went one of two things happened—either riots ensued or revival broke out. It took much courage and perseverance for Paul and his friends to continue in the work of the Lord. Paul was instrumental in teaching the emerging church about Jesus. He has given us teaching letters to help us in our faith journey. Let's look at the Scriptures and learn some lessons about serving the Lord.

Philippians 3:12

Not that I have already obtained all this, or have already been made perfect, but I press on to take hold of that for which Christ Jesus took hold of me.

- Often as believers we feel as though we have to have our lives in a "perfect" place to be useful in serving God. What does this Scripture say about Paul's life and what he was doing about his circumstances? Does this action Paul is applying to his life challenge you? Where can you press in?

Joshua 1:6-9

6 "Be strong and courageous, because you will lead these people to inherit the land I swore to their forefathers to give them. 7 Be strong and very courageous. Be careful to obey all the law my servant Moses gave you; do not turn from it to the right or to the left, that you may be successful wherever you go. 8 Do not let this Book of the Law depart from your mouth; meditate on it day and night, so that you may be careful to do everything written in it. Then you will be prosperous and successful. 9 Have I not commanded you? Be strong and courageous. Do not be terrified; do not be discouraged, for the LORD your God will be with you wherever you go."

- How many times did the Lord tell Joshua to be strong and courageous? Why do you suppose God had to repeat the instruction? List some of the things that God told Joshua would keep him on the right path. How can you implement God's directives?

Hebrews 10:35-39 (NCV)

[35] *So do not lose the courage you had in the past, which has a great reward.* [36] *You must hold on, so you can do what God wants and receive what he has promised.* [37] *For in a very short time, "The One who is coming will come and will not be delayed.* [38] *The person who is right with me will live by trusting in me. But if he turns back with fear, I will not be pleased with him."* [39] *But we are not those who turn back and are lost. We are people who have faith and are saved.*

- If you hold on to your courage, what does God promise? If we trust in God, how does He see us?

1 Corinthians 9:24-25

[24] *Do you not know that in a race all the runners run, but only one gets the prize? Run in such a way as to get the prize.* [25] *Everyone who competes in the games goes into strict training. They do it to get a crown that will not last; but we do it to get a crown that will last forever.*

- Have you ever played competitive sports? What were some of the things you did to prepare yourself for doing your best? Take a moment and write down some things you could pick up or lay down to finish well as a believer.

Hebrews 10:25

Let us not give up meeting together, as some are in the habit of doing, but let us encourage one another—and all the more as you see the Day approaching.

- Why is Christian community so important in your life? Do you remember a time when a friend with faith encouraged you? Can you think of someone now whom you could encourage?

DAILY REFLECTIONS

These are daily reviews of the key Bible verses and related others that will help you think about and apply the insights from this session.

DAY 1
1 Timothy 1:12-13

Strength

12 I thank Christ Jesus our Lord, who has given me strength, that he considered me faithful, appointing me to his service. 13 Even though I was once a blasphemer and a persecutor and a violent man, I was shown mercy because I acted in ignorance and unbelief.

Reflection Question:
Paul was honest about the transformation in his life. Reflect on the transformation Jesus has brought to you.

DAY 2
Acts 11:19, 21

Riots

19 Now those who had been scattered by the persecution in connection with Stephen traveled as far as Phoenicia, Cyprus and Antioch, telling the message only to Jews. 21 The Lord's hand was with them, and a great number of people believed and turned to the Lord.

Reflection Question:
Has your faith in Christ caused any disruption in your world? When have you experienced God's hand on your life?

DAY 3
Acts 13:23-25

Revival

23 "From this man's descendants God has brought to Israel the Savior Jesus, as he promised. 24 Before the coming of Jesus, John preached repentance and baptism to all the people of Israel. 25 As John was completing his work, he said: 'Who do you think I am? I am not that one. No, but he is coming after me, whose sandals I am not worthy to untie.'"

Reflection Question:
Are you conscious of who is looking up to you?

DAY 4

2 Corinthians 11:28

Compassion

Besides everything else, I face daily the pressure of my concern for all the churches.

Reflection Question:
There are burdens we carry and pressures we bear for ourselves and for one another as we seek to obey God. How does your faith grow because of them?

_____

_____

_____

_____

_____

_____

DAY 5

2 Corinthians 2:8-9

Obedience

⁸ I urge you, therefore, to reaffirm your love for him. ⁹ The reason I wrote you was to see if you would stand the test and be obedient in everything.

Reflection Question:
How are you showing your love for your Christ by being obedient in everything?

_____

_____

_____

_____

_____

_____

WEEKLY MEMORY VERSE

⁸ I URGE YOU, THEREFORE, TO REAFFIRM YOUR LOVE FOR HIM. ⁹ THE REASON I WROTE YOU WAS TO SEE IF YOU WOULD STAND THE TEST AND BE OBEDIENT IN EVERYTHING.

2 CORINTHIANS 2:8–9

WEEK 5

INTRODUCTION

When we are first introduced to Saul of Tarsus, he is actively involved with an angry mob that is stoning Stephen for his faith in Jesus (see Acts 7). By the conclusion of the book of Acts, Paul the Apostle is a transformed person. He has become an unrelenting advocate for Jesus of Nazareth as the Christ. God has directed him throughout the Roman world and finally sent him to Rome itself.

CALL TO ROME

Being a Christ-follower is about far more than attending a church or learning a creed. It is a call to "offer ourselves as living sacrifices" and to become ambassadors for the Kingdom of Almighty God. The notion that the God of creation would provide an invitation to participate in His purposes is truly remarkable. A God-assignment brings meaning to the routine of our lives and lifts us above the drudgery. We are reminded that in the smallest tasks— sharing a glass of water—God takes note. We are encouraged to rejoice when people "falsely say all manner of evil against us" because we have a great reward ahead. Serving God adds a dimension of hope and promise to our lives, even when we face challenges.

THE CHURCH

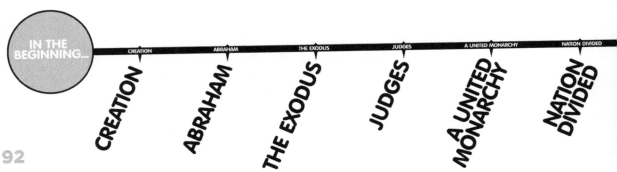

IN THE BEGINNING...

CREATION · ABRAHAM · THE EXODUS · JUDGES · A UNITED MONARCHY · NATION DIVIDED

CREATION

ABRAHAM

THE EXODUS

JUDGES

A UNITED MONARCHY

NATION DIVIDED

GETTING STARTED

Begin the session with a question below or brief activity to become better acquainted with one another.

1 Who is your favorite New Testament character, excluding Jesus?

2 Would you have traveled with Paul? Why or why not?

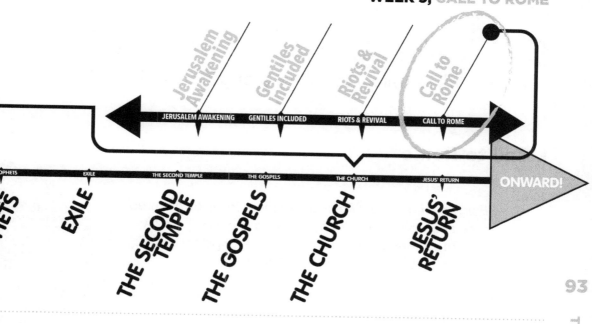

Jerusalem Awakening

Gentiles Included

Riots & Revival

Call to Rome

JERUSALEM AWAKENING   GENTILES INCLUDED   RIOTS & REVIVAL   CALL TO ROME

THE PROPHETS   EXILE   THE SECOND TEMPLE   THE GOSPELS   THE CHURCH   JESUS' RETURN

ONWARD!

THE PROPHETS

EXILE

THE SECOND TEMPLE

THE GOSPELS

THE CHURCH

JESUS' RETURN

OUTLINE OF DVD LESSON

Use the outline below to follow along during the DVD.

I. Call to Rome

Acts 28:30-31

30 For two whole years Paul stayed there in his own rented house and welcomed all who came to see him. 31 Boldly and without hindrance he preached the kingdom of God and taught about the Lord Jesus Christ.

Acts 1:7-8

7 He said to them: "It is not for you to know the times or dates the Father has set by his own authority. 8 But you will receive power when the Holy Spirit comes on you; and you will be my witnesses in Jerusalem, and in all Judea and Samaria, and to the ends of the earth."

II. Paul's Journey to Rome

A. Jerusalem Turmoil

Acts 21:30-32

30 The whole city was aroused, and the people came running from all directions. Seizing Paul, they dragged him from the temple, and immediately the gates were shut. 31 While they were trying to kill him, news reached the commander of the Roman troops that the whole city of Jerusalem was in an uproar. 32 He at once took some officers and soldiers and ran down to the crowd. When the rioters saw the commander and his soldiers, they stopped beating Paul.

B. On board a Ship Bound for Rome

Acts 27:18-20

18 We took such a violent battering from the storm that the next day they began to throw the cargo overboard. 19 On the third day, they threw the ship's tackle overboard with their own hands. 20 When neither sun nor stars appeared for many days and the storm continued raging, we finally gave up all hope of being saved.

C. God Intervenes

Acts 27:23-24

[23] *"Last night an angel of the God whose I am and whom I serve stood beside me* [24] *and said, 'Do not be afraid, Paul. You must stand trial before Caesar; and God has graciously given you the lives of all who sail with you.'"*

III. Losing Hope

A. "Finally Lost All Hope"

B. Hopelessness and Discouragement Are Not God's Intent

C. Defeating Despair

1. Believe God can and wants to provide deliverance.
2. Find a verse of Scripture to fuel your hope.

Hebrews 13:8

Jesus Christ is the same yesterday and today and forever.

3. List two or three things in your life for which you can be thankful.
4. Three times a day stop and read your Scripture out loud and thank God for the good things you can identify.

D. Overcoming Discouragement

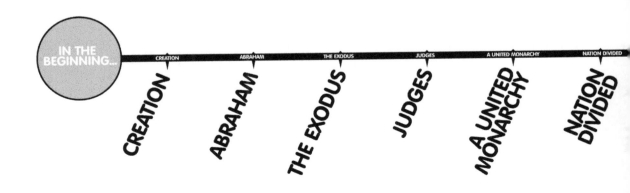

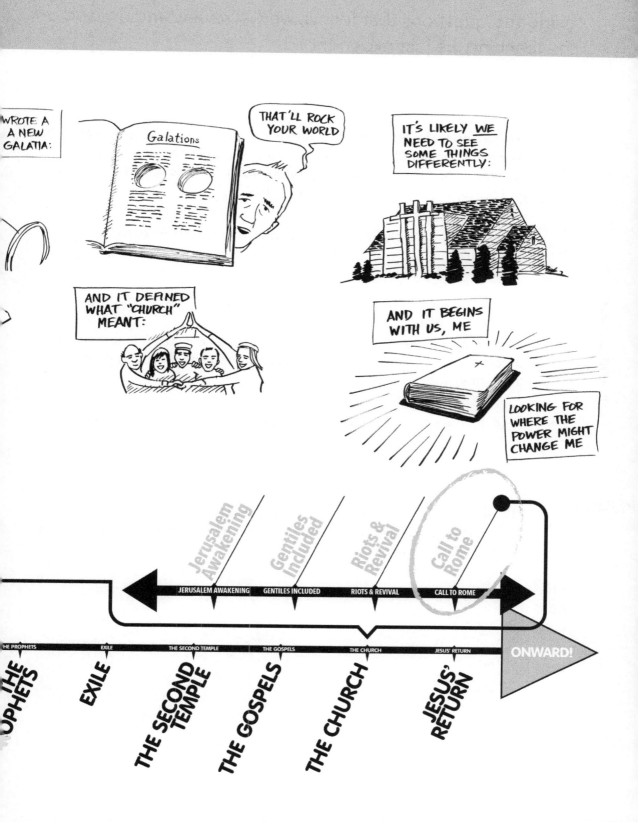

DISCUSSION

Using the questions that follow, we will review and expand on the teaching we just experienced.

Acts 1:7-8

7 He said to them: "It is not for you to know the times or dates the Father has set by his own authority. 8 But you will receive power when the Holy Spirit comes on you; and you will be my witnesses in Jerusalem, and in all Judea and Samaria, and to the ends of the earth."

1 Jesus tells us the Holy Spirit will empower us for a specific purpose. What is it?

Acts 4:13

When they saw the courage of Peter and John and realized that they were unschooled, ordinary men, they were astonished and they took note that these men had been with Jesus.

2 How did the religious leaders in Jerusalem describe Peter and John?

Acts 27:1

When it was decided that we would sail for Italy, Paul and some other prisoners were handed over to a centurion named Julius, who belonged to the Imperial Regiment.

3 Who was Paul's traveling companion to Rome?

Acts 28:3-4

³ *Paul gathered a pile of brushwood and, as he put it on the fire, a viper, driven out by the heat, fastened itself on his hand.* ⁴ *When the islanders saw the snake hanging from his hand, they said to each other, "This man must be a murderer; for though he escaped from the sea, the Justice has not allowed him to live."*

4 After the shipwreck Paul faced yet another challenge. Describe it.

5 How would you describe God's travel arrangements for Paul from Jerusalem to Rome?

99

APPLICATION

Now it's time to make some personal applications of all we've been thinking about in the last few minutes.

READ ALOUD

Scripture is clear—God sent Paul to Rome. However, the details of the trip are surprising. Paul was falsely accused, arrested, survived assassination attempts, and endured multiple trials and even violent storms. God's invitations are not always simple or filled with comfort. We are asked to be faithful followers.

6 Share a time when God led you on a difficult path for His purposes.

Acts 27:9-12

⁹ Much time had been lost, and sailing had already become dangerous because by now it was after the Fast. So Paul warned them, ¹⁰ "Men, I can see that our voyage is going to be disastrous and bring great loss to ship and cargo, and to our own lives also." ¹¹ But the centurion, instead of listening to what Paul said, followed the advice of the pilot and of the owner of the ship. ¹² Since the harbor was unsuitable to winter in, the majority decided that we should sail on, hoping to reach Phoenix and winter there. This was a harbor in Crete, facing both southwest and northwest.

7 What was Paul's warning to the ship's owner? How did the men respond?

21 After the men had gone a long time without food, Paul stood up before them and said: "Men, you should have taken my advice not to sail from Crete; then you would have spared yourselves this damage and loss. 22 But now I urge you to keep up your courage, because not one of you will be lost; only the ship will be destroyed. 23 Last night an angel of the God whose I am and whom I serve stood beside me 24 and said, 'Do not be afraid, Paul. You must stand trial before Caesar; and God has graciously given you the lives of all who sail with you.' 25 So keep up your courage, men, for I have faith in God that it will happen just as he told me. 26 Nevertheless, we must run aground on some island."

8

Paul offered advice a second time, to a more receptive audience. Describe a time when you did not cooperate with God's invitation the first time it was presented.

READ ALOUD

Paul's shipmates faced a fierce struggle with the storm. For more than a week they fought desperately to survive, jettisoning the cargo and forfeiting all profit. Finally, they lost all hope and resigned themselves to destruction. Hopelessness and despair do not arrive in our lives fully formed. They invade a little bit at a time, until finally we are overwhelmed with discouragement and hopelessness. God delivered Paul and his traveling companions. He can deliver us.

9   Our hope is not linked to our present circumstances but to God's power and character. List two or three deliverance stories you know from the Bible.

10   Share a verse of Scripture that has been an encouragement to you.

READ ALOUD

Giving thanks is a powerful spiritual force. It opens our lives to God in new ways and pushes back the spirit of heaviness. We do not ignore the challenges. We choose to turn our attention toward God's present activity and involvement.

11   Take time for each person in the group to share two or three things they are thankful for today.

12   This week, take a moment to share an encouraging verse with one another. A quick call, a text, an email, a social media post—invest a few minutes during the week to share a God-idea.

Discouragement and despair leave us immobilized. Make the effort to give thanks, give and receive encouragement, and open your heart to God's Word. Jesus is the author and completer of our story. What He has begun in your life, He will complete—as you cooperate with Him. Determine today to lay aside complaining and dissatisfaction and to become a grateful person focused on the promises of a living God.

13 Share a circumstance you are trusting God for today.

103

PRAYER

Close the session in prayer. Share prayer requests with the group, and pray for each other. Close by praying the following prayer together.

Heavenly Father, I rejoice today that You are watching over my life. I rest in the shadow of Your strength and power. Through the blood of Jesus Christ I have been redeemed out of the hand of the devil; through the blood of Jesus all my sins are forgiven. My body is a temple of the Holy Spirit, redeemed and cleansed by the blood of Jesus. Therefore Satan has no place in me and no power over me, through the blood of Jesus. I rejoice in this great victory You have given to me. You are my hope and my Redeemer. In Jesus' name, amen.

Prayer requests this week:

GOING DEEPER

This section is designed to do as homework, if you choose, between your Small Group meetings.

Acts 16:16-34

16 Once when we were going to the place of prayer, we were met by a slave girl who had a spirit by which she predicted the future. She earned a great deal of money for her owners by fortune-telling. 17 This girl followed Paul and the rest of us, shouting, "These men are servants of the Most High God, who are telling you the way to be saved." 18 She kept this up for many days. Finally Paul became so troubled that he turned around and said to the spirit, "In the name of Jesus Christ I command you to come out of her!" At that moment the spirit left her. 19 When the owners of the slave girl realized that their hope of making money was gone, they seized Paul and Silas and dragged them into the marketplace to face the authorities. 20 They brought them before the magistrates and said, "These men are Jews, and are throwing our city into an uproar 21 by advocating customs unlawful for us Romans to accept or practice." 22 The crowd joined in the attack against Paul and Silas, and the magistrates ordered them to be stripped and beaten. 23 After they had been severely flogged, they were thrown into prison, and the jailer was commanded to guard them carefully. 24 Upon receiving such orders, he put them in the inner cell and fastened their feet in the stocks. 25 About midnight Paul and Silas were praying and singing hymns to God, and the other prisoners were listening to them. 26 Suddenly there was such a violent earthquake that the foundations of the prison were shaken. At once all the prison doors flew open, and everybody's chains came loose. 27 The jailer woke up, and when he saw the prison doors open, he drew his sword and was about to kill himself because he thought the prisoners had escaped. 28 But Paul shouted, "Don't harm yourself! We are all here!" 29 The jailer called for lights, rushed in and fell trembling before Paul and Silas. 30 He then brought them out and asked, "Sirs, what must I do to be saved?" 31 They replied, "Believe in the Lord Jesus, and you will be saved—you and your household." 32 Then they spoke the word of the Lord to him and to all the others in his house. 33 At that hour of the night the jailer took them and washed their wounds; then immediately he and all his family were baptized. 34 The jailer brought them into his house and set a meal before them; he was filled with joy because he had come to believe in God—he and his whole family.

Paul had a vision from the Lord to go and help the people of Macedonia. In obedience he and Silas went and told the good news of Jesus where many were saved, baptized, and delivered. It was a successful trip, but they were met with great opposition. They suffered harassment, severe beatings, and even jail. Paul understood that serving the Lord was not always about comfort and ease. He was passionate and dedicated to the cause of Christ even if that meant death. Let's review the story and see how Paul and Silas honored the Lord.

Read vv. 16-19.

- Where were Paul and Silas going? Whom did they encounter?

- What was their response?

- Why were the slave owners angry?

- Have you ever done the right thing and did not get a favorable response? How did you handle it?

Read vv. 20-27.

- Paul and Silas were falsely accused by the slave girl's owners. What quickly followed?

- What was the response of Paul and Silas? What was the result? Who was listening?

- Describe a time you chose to give thanks instead of sinking into your feelings.

- Are you currently going through a difficult time? Take a moment to think of a favorite worship song or hymn you could offer to God, then sing it to Him.

Read vv. 28-34.

- A terrified jailer woke up to hear Paul say, "We are all here." What was the result of Paul and Silas remaining in prison?

- Have you ever remained in a difficult place to honor the Lord? What prepared you for the task?

- How many of the jailer's household were saved?

- In your opinion, what was the price of revival in Philippi?

DAILY REFLECTIONS

These are daily reviews of the key Bible verses and related others that will help you think about and apply the insights from this session.

DAY 1
Acts 1:8
Receive Power

"But you will receive power when the Holy Spirit comes on you; and you will be my witnesses in Jerusalem, and in all Judea and Samaria, and to the ends of the earth."

Reflection Question:
Have you intentionally embraced the Holy Spirit for the kind of boldness that Paul says Jesus spoke about before He was taken up from their sight? How important do you think this instruction was? What will the Holy Spirit empower you for?

DAY 2
Acts 26:16-17
Get Up

16 "'Now get up and stand on your feet. I have appeared to you to appoint you as a servant and as a witness of what you have seen of me and what I will show you. 17 I will rescue you from your own people and from the Gentiles. I am sending you to them.'"

Reflection Question:
What is God's promise to Paul? How does God's promise to Paul bring hope to your circumstances?

DAY 3
Philippians 1:3-6
God's Work in Us

3 I thank my God every time I remember you. 4 In all my prayers for all of you, I always pray with joy 5 because of your partnership in the gospel from the first day until now, 6 being confident of this, that he who began a good work in you will carry it on to completion until the day of Christ Jesus.

Reflective Question:
How important are our prayers for one another? What is a good work God has begun in you?

DAY 4

Ephesians 6:19-20

Ambassadors

^{19} Pray also for me, that whenever I speak, words may be given me so that I will fearlessly make known the mystery of the gospel, ^{20} for which I am an ambassador in chains. Pray that I may declare it fearlessly, as I should.

Reflection Question:
Paul was an ambassador in chains. Take a moment and thank God that He will use your life in spite of limits.

_____

_____

_____

_____

_____

DAY 5

Philippians 2:14-16

Shine like Stars

^{14} Do everything without complaining or arguing, ^{15} so that you may become blameless and pure, children of God without fault in a crooked and depraved generation, in which you shine like stars in the universe ^{16} as you hold out the word of life— in order that I may boast on the day of Christ that I did not run or labor for nothing.

Reflection Question:
Think of some of the positive outcomes of refraining from grumbling and arguing. Who in your sphere of friends has been a good example for you in this area?

_____

_____

_____

WEEKLY MEMORY VERSE

"BUT YOU WILL RECEIVE POWER WHEN THE HOLY SPIRIT COMES ON YOU; AND YOU WILL BE MY WITNESSES IN JERUSALEM, AND IN ALL JUDEA AND SAMARIA, AND TO THE ENDS OF THE EARTH."

ACTS 1:8

WEEK 6

INTRODUCTION

The book of Revelation is a special book, an entire book of prophecy. God cares enough about us to provide insight into a most critical season of human history. He does not want us to be unprepared or surprised. It is a book of tremendous hope, describing the return of our Lord. Jesus is coming back to deliver His people from this current evil age.

REVELATION

The message of Revelation is so important it required a most trusted friend to be the recipient. It should not be surprising the insight was delivered to the Apostle John, Jesus' most trusted disciple. John had been exiled to Patmos. His peers were gone. He had invested his life in telling others about the most remarkable man he ever knew, Jesus. Then one day, on the Lord's day, John heard a voice—a familiar voice. He turned to look and saw Jesus. He fell at His feet. The book of Revelation is the message Jesus wanted us to have about His return. He trusted John to relay it to us. What a privilege we have to serve a Lord who demonstrates such concern about our preparedness.

THE CHURCH

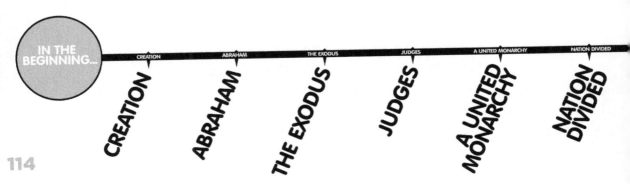

IN THE BEGINNING...

CREATION

ABRAHAM

THE EXODUS

JUDGES

A UNITED MONARCHY

NATION DIVIDED

114

GETTING STARTED

Begin the session with a question below or brief activity to become better acquainted with one another.

1 Share one thing you have learned during *The Whiteboard Bible* study.

2 As a group, try to list the books of the New Testament in their proper order.

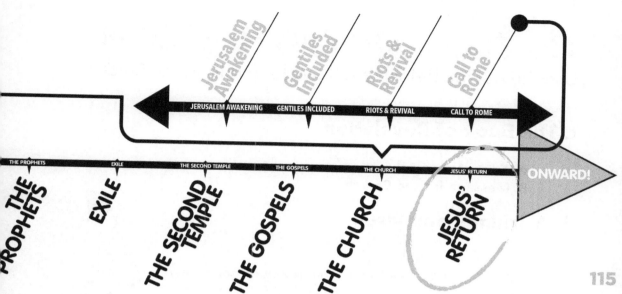

AFTER JESUS ASCENDED, JOHN WAS EXILED TO AN ISLAND CALLED PATMOS

WHILE THERE, GOD GAVE HIM A GREAT VISION WHICH HE RECORDED — REVELATION

OUTLINE OF DVD LESSON

Use the outline below to follow along during the DVD.

I. The Book of Revelation

A. Entrusted to John
B. Message for the Church

II. A Triumphant Jesus

Revelation 1:17-19

¹⁷ When I saw him, I fell at his feet as though dead. Then he placed his right hand on me and said: "Do not be afraid. I am the First and the Last. ¹⁸ I am the Living One; I was dead, and behold I am alive for ever and ever! And I hold the keys of death and Hades. ¹⁹ Write, therefore, what you have seen, what is now and what will take place later."

A. Jesus' First Instruction—"Do Not Be Afraid"

B. "The Living One"

C. Message for the Church—Overcome

Revelation 21:7-8

⁷ "He who overcomes will inherit all this, and I will be his God and he will be my son. ⁸ But the cowardly, the unbelieving, the vile, the murderers, the sexually immoral, those who practice magic arts, the idolaters and all liars—their place will be in the fiery lake of burning sulfur. This is the second death."

D. Jesus Is Victorious!

116

THE WHITEBOARD BIBLE

III. Fear

A. Consistent Message from God to Us—"Fear Not"
B. The Key to Defeating Fear—"Trust"

Psalm 56:11
In God I trust; I will not be afraid.

JOHN'S WRITING DESCRIBES WHAT WILL HAPPEN WHEN JESUS RETURNS

A MIGHTY SOURCE
REVELATION

THE LAST PAGE IN YOUR BIBLE IS FROM "REVELATION"

REVELATION WAS WRITTEN BY JOHN, JESUS' BEST FRIEND

REVEL... FULL ... AND S...

WE'VE COME TO THE END OF OUR STORY

ROAD ENDS

AFTER JESUS ASCENDED, JOHN WAS EXILED TO AN ISLAND CALLED PATMOS

WHILE T... GAVE H... VISION RECORD...

THE CHURCH

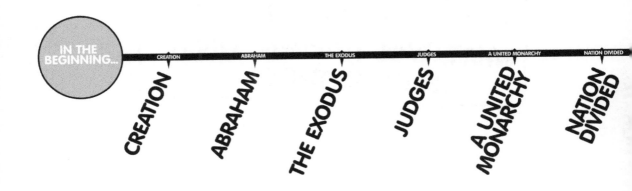

IN THE BEGINNING...

CREATION

ABRAHAM

THE EXODUS

JUDGES

A UNITED MONARCHY

NATION DIVIDED

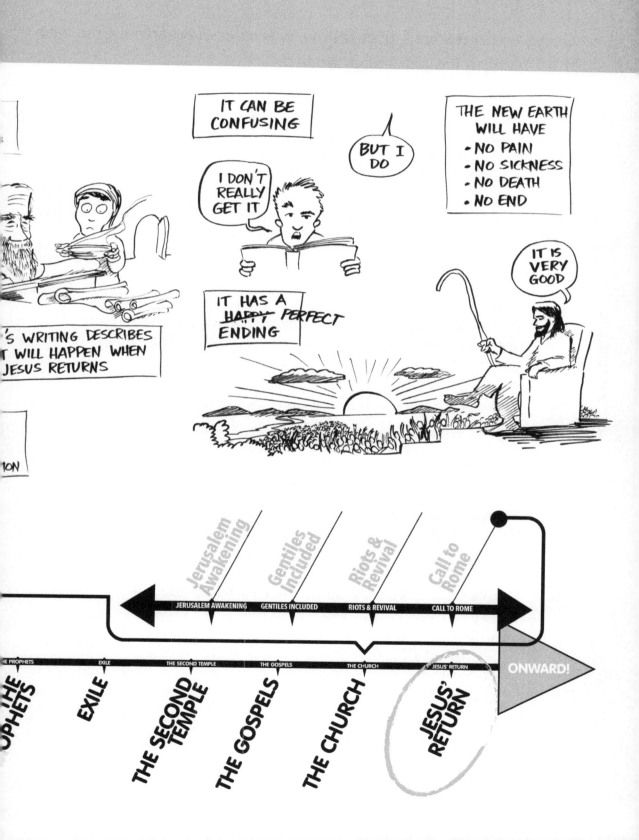

DISCUSSION

Using the questions that follow, we will review and expand on the teaching we just experienced.

Revelation 1:18

"I am the Living One; I was dead, and behold, I am alive for ever and ever! And I hold the keys of death and Hades."

1 When Jesus is introduced in the Gospels, He is a vulnerable baby. When we meet Jesus in Revelation, He holds which keys?

Revelation 1:1

The revelation from Jesus Christ, which God gave him to show his servants what must soon take place. He made it known by sending his angel to his servant John.

2 The book of Revelation is a revelation concerning a specific person. Who is it?

Revelation 1:3

Blessed is the one who reads the words of this prophecy, and blessed are those who hear it and take to heart what is written in it, because the time is near.

3 How do we secure the blessing promised in this Revelation?

4   How is Jesus different in Revelation from in the Gospels?

5   Describe John's circumstances when we meet him in Revelation.

APPLICATION

Now it's time to make some personal applications of all we've been thinking about in the last few minutes.

....

READ ALOUD

Revelation begins with John's vision of Jesus. We are invited to witness a remarkable reunion between friends. Jesus has some very direct words for John. They are insightful for us in preparing for what is ahead. Pay close attention to what Jesus said.

Revelation 1:17-19

17 When I saw him, I fell at his feet as though dead. Then he placed his right hand on me and said: "Do not be afraid. I am the First and the Last. 18 I am the Living One; I was dead, and behold I am alive for ever and ever! And I hold the keys of death and Hades. 19 "Write, therefore, what you have seen, what is now and what will take place later."

6 What was Jesus' first instruction? Good news: if Jesus says "do not" it means we can be free of this.

7 Jesus says "I am" three times. List the three "I am" statements. What do these tell us about Jesus' power and authority?

1 Corinthians 15:26

The last enemy to be destroyed is death.

READ ALOUD

For Jesus to hold the keys of death and Hades suggests a victory. The last enemy has been defeated. Jesus is absolute victor. In Revelation we see Jesus as conqueror, judge, and king. His judgment is delivered in the earth. His kingdom comes in fullness. His followers are delivered completely. In Revelation, Jesus is intervening on behalf of His followers, not extending an invitation.

Romans 10:9-13

⁹ That if you confess with your mouth, "Jesus is Lord," and believe in your heart that God raised him from the dead, you will be saved. ¹⁰ For it is with your heart that you believe and are justified, and it is with your mouth that you confess and are saved. ¹¹ As Scripture says, "Anyone who trusts in him will never be put to shame." ¹² For there is no difference between Jew and Gentile—the same Lord is Lord of all and richly blesses all who call on him, ¹³ for, "Everyone who calls on the name of the Lord will be saved."

8 Take a moment and review how to become a participant in the Kingdom of God.

123

THE WHITEBOARD BIBLE

THE NEW EARTH
WILL HAVE
- NO PAIN
- NO SICKNESS
- NO DEATH
- NO END

9 Take a few minutes for one or two of the group to briefly share your journey of becoming a Christ-follower.

> **Revelation 21:7-8**
>
> [7] "He who overcomes will inherit all this, and I will be his God and he will be my son. [8] But the cowardly, the unbelieving, the vile, the murderers, the sexually immoral, those who practice magic arts, the idolaters and all liars—their place will be in the fiery lake of burning sulfur. This is the second death."

10 What is necessary to inherit all that is described in Revelation?

11 Eight characteristics are listed of those whose destiny is the "fiery lake." List the opposite of those eight characteristics.

1) cowardly—courageous
2) unbelieving—
3) vile—
4) murderers—
5) sexually immoral—
6) practitioners of magic arts—
7) idolaters—
8) all liars—

READ ALOUD

These antonyms provide a character guide for overcomers. Allowing the character of the King to be formed within us brings deliverance. Overcoming is not the result of a singular heroic act, but rather the outcome of cooperating with the Spirit of God in allowing obedience to the King to fill your life.

12 Discuss ways to demonstrate the character traits of the overcomers; i.e., how do we display courage as Christ-followers?

Psalm 56:11

In God I trust; I will not be afraid.

13 Fear paralyzes. Trust empowers. Describe a way in which you have learned to trust God.

Revelation 22:20-21

²⁰ He who testifies to these things says, "Yes, I am coming soon." Amen. Come, Lord Jesus. ²¹ The grace of the Lord Jesus be with God's people. Amen.

Matthew 24:14

And this gospel of the kingdom will be preached in the whole world as a testimony to all nations, and then the end will come.

14 What can we do to facilitate the soon return of Jesus?

PRAYER

Close the session in prayer. Share prayer requests with the group, and pray for each other. Close by praying the following prayer together.

Heavenly Father, thank You for providing the help of the Holy Spirit. Open my eyes to see and my ears to listen. Help me to recognize the signs of this season that I may complete the course You have created me for. I choose to yield to You in obedience and to turn away from all ungodliness. Give me boldness to embrace the truth, the courage to persevere, and the strength to stand. May Jesus be glorified through my life. In Jesus' name, amen.

Prayer requests this week:

_____

_____

_____

_____

_____

GOING DEEPER

This section is designed to do as homework, if you choose, between your Small Group meetings.

....

Revelation 3:14-22

To the Church in Laodicea

14 "To the angel of the church in Laodicea write: These are the words of the Amen, the faithful and true witness, the ruler of God's creation. 15 I know your deeds, that you are neither cold nor hot. I wish you were either one or the other! 16 So, because you are lukewarm—neither hot nor cold—I am about to spit you out of my mouth. 17 You say, 'I am rich; I have acquired wealth and do not need a thing.' But you do not realize that you are wretched, pitiful, poor, blind and naked. 18 I counsel you to buy from me gold refined in the fire, so you can become rich; and white clothes to wear, so you can cover your shameful nakedness; and salve to put on your eyes, so you can see. 19 Those whom I love I rebuke and discipline. So be earnest, and repent. 20 Here I am! I stand at the door and knock. If anyone hears my voice and opens the door, I will come in and eat with him, and he with me. 21 To him who overcomes, I will give the right to sit with me on my throne, just as I overcame and sat down with my Father on his throne. 22 He who has an ear, let him hear what the Spirit says to the churches."

- In Revelation 2 and 3 Jesus has messages for seven churches. He instructs John to tell them what will give them the ability to overcome. Let's look at the church in Laodicea and discover what we can learn from their message.

Read vv. 14-16.

- What does Jesus tell the church about their deeds? What is He warning them He will do? It takes embracing the Holy Spirit and a passion to serve others to be effective and useful. Describe some ways you are embracing the Holy Spirit and serving others.

Read vv. 17-18.

- The Laodicean church was materially wealthy and arrogant and without the ability to see their true need. What truth about their position does Jesus reveal? What does He counsel them to buy?

- Compared to other cultures how would you describe your own in terms of wealth? How are we vulnerable to self-sufficiency and pride? What things take precedence in your schedule and budget? How could you begin to offer yourself for refinement and cleansing?

Read vv. 19-22.

- What does Jesus promise the one who welcomes him? What does He promise for those who are victorious over sin?

DAILY REFLECTIONS

These are daily reviews of the key Bible verses and related others that will help you think about and apply the insights from this session.

DAY 1

Revelation 1:8

I Am

"I am the Alpha and the Omega," says the Lord God, "who is, and who was, and who is to come, the Almighty."

Reflection Question:
Is God the first and the last thought in your day? How often do you think about His coming?

DAY 2

Psalm 34:15-16

Eyes of the Lord

15 The eyes of the LORD are on the righteous and his ears are attentive to their cry; 16 the face of the LORD is against those who do evil, to cut off the memory of them from the earth.

Reflection Question:
To whom is the Lord attentive?

DAY 3

Isaiah 24:21-23

Great Glory

21 In that day the LORD will punish the powers in the heavens above and the kings on the earth below. 22 They will be herded together like prisoners bound in a dungeon; they will be shut up in prison and be punished after many days. 23 The moon will be abashed, the sun ashamed; for the LORD Almighty will reign on Mount Zion and in Jerusalem, and before its elders, gloriously.

Reflection Question:
What will happen to darkness when the Lord reigns in great glory?

DAY 4

Isaiah 26:2-3

Trust in the Lord

² *Open the gates that the righteous nation may enter, the nation that keeps faith.* ³ *You will keep in perfect peace him whose mind is steadfast, because he trusts in you.*

Reflection Question:
How do you keep your mind steadfast?

DAY 5

Isaiah 35:3-4

Do Not Fear

³ *Strengthen the feeble hands, steady the knees that give way;* ⁴ *say to those with fearful hearts, "Be strong, do not fear; your God will come, he will come with vengeance; with divine retribution he will come to save you."*

Reflection Question:
God wants you to be strengthened and steady without fear. What have you learned from this study to encourage you?

WEEKLY MEMORY VERSE

"I AM THE ALPHA AND THE OMEGA," SAYS THE LORD GOD, "WHO IS, AND WHO WAS, AND WHO IS TO COME, THE ALMIGHTY."

REVELATION 1:8

APPENDIX

FREQUENTLY ASKED QUESTIONS

What do we do on the first night of our group?
Like all fun things in life—have a party! A "get to know you" coffee, dinner, or dessert is a great way to launch a new study. You may want to review the Small Group Agreement and share the names of a few friends you can invite to join you. But most important, have fun before your study time begins.

Where do we find new members for our group?
We encourage you to pray with your group and then brainstorm a list of people from work, church, your neighborhood, your children's school, family, the gym, and so forth. Then have each group member invite several of the people on his or her list.

How long will this group meet?
It's totally up to the group—once you come to the end of this six-week study. Most groups meet weekly for at least their first six weeks, but every other week can work as well.

At the end of this study, each group member may decide if he or she wants to continue on for another six-week study. Some groups launch relationships for years to come, and others are stepping stones into another group experience. Either way, enjoy the journey.

What if this group is not working for us?

You're not alone! This could be the result of a personality conflict, life stage difference, geographical distance, level of spiritual maturity, or any number of things. Relax. Pray for God's direction, and at the end of this six-week study, decide whether to continue with this group or find another. You don't buy the first car you look at or marry the first person you date, and the same goes with a group. Don't bail out before the 6 weeks are up—God might have something to teach you. Also, don't run from conflict or prejudge people before you have given them a chance. God is still working in you too!

How do we handle the childcare needs in our group?

We suggest that you empower the group to openly brainstorm solutions. You may try one option that works for a while and then adjust over time. Our favorite approach is for adults to meet in the living room and to share the cost of a babysitter (or two) who can be with the kids in a different part of the house. In this way, parents don't have to be away from their children all evening when their children are too young to be left at home. A second option is to use one home for the kids and a second home (close by or a phone call away) for the adults. A third idea is to rotate the responsibility of providing a lesson or care for the children either in the same home or in another home nearby. This can be an incredible blessing for kids. Finally, the most common idea is to decide that you need to have a night to invest in your spiritual lives and to make your own arrangements for child care. No matter what decision the group makes, the best approach is to dialogue openly about both the problem and the solution.

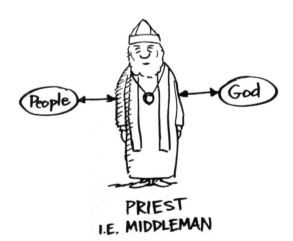

PRIEST
I.E. MIDDLEMAN

SMALL GROUP AGREEMENT

Our Expectations:

To provide a predictable environment where participants experience authentic community and spiritual growth.

Group Attendance	We would like for everyone to make it a priority to attend each week.
Safe Environment	To help create a safe place where people can be heard and feel loved.
Respect Differences	To be gentle and gracious to fellow group members with different spiritual maturity, personal opinions, temperaments, or "imperfections." We are all works in progress.
Confidentiality	To keep anything that is shared strictly confidential and within the group, and to avoid sharing improper information about those outside the group.
Encouragement for Growth	To be not just takers but givers of life. We want to spiritually multiply our lives by serving others with our God-given gifts.
Shared Ownership	To remember that every member is a minister and to ensure that each attender will share a small team role or responsibility over time (i.e. bringing food or closing in prayer).
Rotating Hosts/ Leaders and Homes	To encourage different people to host the group in their homes, and to rotate the responsibility of facilitating each meeting (see the Small Group Calendar).

Our Times Together:

- Refreshments _____
- Childcare _____
- When we will meet (day of week) _____
- Where we will meet (place) _____
- We will begin at (time) _____ and end at _____
- We will do our best to have some or all of us attend a worship service together.
  Our primary worship service time will be _____

SMALL GROUP CALENDAR

Planning and calendaring can help ensure the greatest participation at every meeting. Be sure to include birthdays, socials, church events, holidays, and projects.

DATE	LESSON	HOST HOME	REFRESHMENTS	LEADER
MONDAY JAN 15	1	BILL	JOE	BILL

MEMORY VERSES

Week 1

[6] "He is not here; he has risen! Remember how he told you, while he was still with you in Galilee: [7] 'The Son of Man must be delivered into the hands of sinful men, be crucified and on the third day be raised again.'"
Luke 24:6-7

Week 2

[19] "Repent, then, and turn to God, so that your sins may be wiped out, that times of refreshing may come from the Lord, [20] and that he may send the Christ, who has been appointed for you—even Jesus."
Acts 3:19-20

Week 3

"Salvation is found in no one else, for there is no other name under heaven given to men by which we must be saved."
Acts 4:12

Week 4

[8] I urge you, therefore, to reaffirm your love for him. [9] The reason I wrote you was to see if you would stand the test and be obedient in everything.
2 Corinthians 2:8-9

Week 5

"But you will receive power when the Holy Spirit comes on you; and you will be my witnesses in Jerusalem, and in all Judea and Samaria, and to the ends of the earth."
Acts 1:8

Week 6

"I am the Alpha and the Omega," says the Lord God, "who is, and who was, and who is to come, the Almighty."
Revelation 1:8

PRAYER AND PRAISE REPORT

	Prayer Requests	Praise Reports
Week 1		
Week 2		
Week 3		
Week 4		
Week 5		
Week 6		

NOTES

One-Year Bible Reading Plan

Week 1
- ☐ Gen. 1-3
- ☐ Gen. 4-7
- ☐ Gen. 8-11
- ☐ Gen. 12-15
- ☐ Gen. 16-18
- ☐ Gen. 19-21
- ☐ Gen. 22-24

Week 2
- ☐ Gen. 25-26
- ☐ Gen. 27-29
- ☐ Gen. 30-31
- ☐ Gen. 32-34
- ☐ Gen. 35-37
- ☐ Gen. 38-40
- ☐ Gen. 41-42

Week 3
- ☐ Gen. 43-45
- ☐ Gen. 46-47
- ☐ Gen. 48-50
- ☐ Exod. 1-3
- ☐ Exod. 4-6
- ☐ Exod. 7-9
- ☐ Exod. 10-12

Week 4
- ☐ Exod. 13-15
- ☐ Exod. 16-18
- ☐ Exod. 19-21
- ☐ Exod. 22-24
- ☐ Exod. 25-27
- ☐ Exod. 28-29
- ☐ Exod. 30-32

Week 5
- ☐ Exod. 33-35
- ☐ Exod. 36-38
- ☐ Exod. 39-40
- ☐ Lev. 1-4
- ☐ Lev. 5-7
- ☐ Lev. 8-10
- ☐ Lev. 11-13

Week 6
- ☐ Lev. 14-15
- ☐ Lev. 16-17
- ☐ Lev. 18-19
- ☐ Lev. 20-21
- ☐ Lev. 22-23
- ☐ Lev. 24-25
- ☐ Lev. 26-27

Week 7
- ☐ Num. 1-4
- ☐ Num. 5-6
- ☐ Num. 7
- ☐ Num. 8-10
- ☐ Num. 11-13
- ☐ Num. 14-15
- ☐ Num. 16-17

Week 8
- ☐ Num. 18-20
- ☐ Num. 21-22
- ☐ Num. 23-25
- ☐ Num. 26-27
- ☐ Num. 28-30
- ☐ Num. 31-33
- ☐ Num. 34-36

Week 9
- ☐ Deut. 1
- ☐ Deut. 2
- ☐ Deut. 3-4
- ☐ Deut. 5-7
- ☐ Deut. 8-10
- ☐ Deut. 11-13
- ☐ Deut. 14-16

Week 10
- ☐ Deut. 17-19
- ☐ Deut. 20-22
- ☐ Deut. 23-25
- ☐ Deut. 26-27
- ☐ Deut. 28-30
- ☐ Deut. 31-32
- ☐ Deut. 33-34

Week 11
- ☐ Josh. 1-4
- ☐ Josh. 5-8
- ☐ Josh. 9-12
- ☐ Josh. 13-16
- ☐ Josh. 17-20
- ☐ Josh. 21-22
- ☐ Josh. 23-24

Week 12
- ☐ Judg. 1-4
- ☐ Judg. 5-7
- ☐ Judg. 8-10
- ☐ Judg. 11-14
- ☐ Judg. 15-18
- ☐ Judg. 19-21
- ☐ Ruth

Week 13
- ☐ 1 Sam. 1-4
- ☐ 1 Sam. 5-10
- ☐ 1 Sam. 11-14
- ☐ 1 Sam. 15-17
- ☐ 1 Sam. 18-21
- ☐ 1 Sam. 22-25
- ☐ 1 Sam. 26-31

Week 14
- ☐ 2 Sam. 1-4
- ☐ 2 Sam. 5-8
- ☐ 2 Sam. 9-12
- ☐ 2 Sam. 13-15
- ☐ 2 Sam. 16-18
- ☐ 2 Sam. 19-21
- ☐ 2 Sam. 22-24

Week 15
- ☐ 1 Kgs. 1-3
- ☐ 1 Kgs. 4-6
- ☐ 1 Kgs. 7-8
- ☐ 1 Kgs. 9-11
- ☐ 1 Kgs. 12-15
- ☐ 1 Kgs. 16-19
- ☐ 1 Kgs. 20-22

Week 16
- [ ] 2 Kgs. 1-4
- [ ] 2 Kgs. 5-8
- [ ] 2 Kgs. 9-11
- [ ] 2 Kgs. 12-15
- [ ] 2 Kgs. 16-18
- [ ] 2 Kgs. 19-22
- [ ] 2 Kgs. 23-25

Week 17
- [ ] 1 Chron. 1-2
- [ ] 1 Chron. 3-5
- [ ] 1 Chron. 6-7
- [ ] 1 Chron. 8-10
- [ ] 1 Chron. 11-17
- [ ] 1 Chron. 18-23
- [ ] 1 Chron. 24-26

Week 18
- [ ] 1 Chron. 27-29
- [ ] 2 Chron. 1-5
- [ ] 2 Chron. 6-9
- [ ] 2 Chron. 10-15
- [ ] 2 Chron. 16-20
- [ ] 2 Chron. 21-25
- [ ] 2 Chron. 26-29

Week 19
- [ ] 2 Chron. 30-32
- [ ] 2 Chron. 33-36
- [ ] Ezra 1-3
- [ ] Ezra 4-7
- [ ] Ezra 8-10
- [ ] Neh. 1-5
- [ ] Neh. 6-7

Week 20
- [ ] Neh. 8-10
- [ ] Neh. 11-13
- [ ] Est. 1-5
- [ ] Est. 6-10
- [ ] Job 1-5
- [ ] Job 6-9
- [ ] Job 10-13

Week 21
- [ ] Job 14-18
- [ ] Job 19-22
- [ ] Job 23-28
- [ ] Job 29-32
- [ ] Job 33-36
- [ ] Job 37-39
- [ ] Job 40-42

Week 22
- [ ] Ps. 1-9
- [ ] Ps. 10-17
- [ ] Ps. 18
- [ ] Ps. 19-22
- [ ] Ps. 23-29
- [ ] Ps. 30-34
- [ ] Ps. 35-39

Week 23
- [ ] Ps. 40-46
- [ ] Ps. 47-54
- [ ] Ps. 55-61
- [ ] Ps. 62-68
- [ ] Ps. 69-73
- [ ] Ps. 74-77
- [ ] Ps. 78-80

Week 24
- [ ] Ps. 81-87
- [ ] Ps. 88-91
- [ ] Ps. 92-100
- [ ] Ps. 101-104
- [ ] Ps. 105-106
- [ ] Ps. 107-110
- [ ] Ps. 111-118

Week 25
- [ ] Ps. 119:1-88
- [ ] Ps. 119:89-176
- [ ] Ps. 120-125
- [ ] Ps. 126-132
- [ ] Ps. 133-139
- [ ] Ps. 140-145
- [ ] Ps. 146-150

Week 26
- [ ] Prov. 1-3
- [ ] Prov. 4-6
- [ ] Prov. 7-10
- [ ] Prov. 11-14
- [ ] Prov. 15-17
- [ ] Prov. 18-20
- [ ] Prov. 21-23

Week 27
- [ ] Prov. 24-26
- [ ] Prov. 27-29
- [ ] Prov. 30-31
- [ ] Eccles. 1-4
- [ ] Eccles. 5-8
- [ ] Eccles. 9-12
- [ ] Song

Week 28
- [ ] Isa. 1-4
- [ ] Isa. 5-8
- [ ] Isa. 9-13
- [ ] Isa. 14-19
- [ ] Isa. 20-24
- [ ] Isa. 25-29
- [ ] Isa. 30-33

Week 29
- [ ] Isa. 34-37
- [ ] Isa. 38-41
- [ ] Isa. 42-45
- [ ] Isa. 46-51
- [ ] Isa. 52-57
- [ ] Isa. 58-61
- [ ] Isa. 62-66

Week 30
- [ ] Jer. 1-4
- [ ] Jer. 5-9
- [ ] Jer. 10-13
- [ ] Jer. 14-17
- [ ] Jer. 18-22
- [ ] Jer. 23-25
- [ ] Jer. 26-29

Week 31
- ☐ Jer. 30-31
- ☐ Jer. 32-34
- ☐ Jer. 35-37
- ☐ Jer. 38-41
- ☐ Jer. 42-45
- ☐ Jer. 46-48
- ☐ Jer. 49-52

Week 32
- ☐ Lam. 1-2
- ☐ Lam. 3-5
- ☐ Ezek. 1-2
- ☐ Ezek. 3-5
- ☐ Ezek. 6-8
- ☐ Ezek. 9-12
- ☐ Ezek. 13-15

Week 33
- ☐ Ezek. 16-17
- ☐ Ezek. 18-20
- ☐ Ezek. 21-22
- ☐ Ezek. 23-24
- ☐ Ezek. 25-27
- ☐ Ezek. 28-30
- ☐ Ezek. 31-33

Week 34
- ☐ Ezek. 34-36
- ☐ Ezek. 37-39
- ☐ Ezek. 40-42
- ☐ Ezek. 43-45
- ☐ Ezek. 46-48
- ☐ Dan. 1-3
- ☐ Dan. 4-6

Week 35
- ☐ Dan. 7-9
- ☐ Dan. 10-12
- ☐ Hos. 1-7
- ☐ Hos. 8-14
- ☐ Joel
- ☐ Amos 1-5
- ☐ Amos 6-9

Week 36
- ☐ Obad.-Jon.
- ☐ Mic.-Nah.
- ☐ Hab.-Zeph.
- ☐ Hag.
- ☐ Zech. 1-7
- ☐ Zech. 8-14
- ☐ Mal.

Week 37
- ☐ Matt. 1-2
- ☐ Matt. 3-4
- ☐ Matt. 5-6
- ☐ Matt. 7-8
- ☐ Matt. 9-10
- ☐ Matt. 11-12
- ☐ Matt. 13-14

Week 38
- ☐ Matt. 15-17
- ☐ Matt. 18-19
- ☐ Matt. 20-21
- ☐ Matt. 22-23
- ☐ Matt. 24-25
- ☐ Matt. 26
- ☐ Matt. 27-28

Week 39
- ☐ Mark 1-3
- ☐ Mark 4-5
- ☐ Mark 6-7
- ☐ Mark 8-9
- ☐ Mark 10-11
- ☐ Mark 12-14
- ☐ Mark 15-16

Week 40
- ☐ Luke 1
- ☐ Luke 2
- ☐ Luke 3
- ☐ Luke 4-5
- ☐ Luke 6-7
- ☐ Luke 8-9
- ☐ Luke 10-11

Week 41
- ☐ Luke 12-13
- ☐ Luke 14-15
- ☐ Luke 16
- ☐ Luke 17-18
- ☐ Luke 19-20
- ☐ Luke 21-22
- ☐ Luke 23-24

Week 42
- ☐ John 1-3
- ☐ John 4-7
- ☐ John 8-10
- ☐ John 11-13
- ☐ John 14-17
- ☐ John 18-19
- ☐ John 20-21

Week 43
- ☐ Acts 1-2
- ☐ Acts 3
- ☐ Acts 4-6
- ☐ Acts 7-8
- ☐ Acts 9-10
- ☐ Acts 11-13
- ☐ Acts 14-15

Week 44
- ☐ Acts 16-17
- ☐ Acts 18-20
- ☐ Acts 21-23
- ☐ Acts 24-26
- ☐ Acts 27-28
- ☐ Rom. 1-3
- ☐ Rom. 4-7

Week 45
- ☐ Rom. 8-10
- ☐ Rom. 11-13
- ☐ Rom. 14-16
- ☐ 1 Cor. 1-4
- ☐ 1 Cor. 5-8
- ☐ 1 Cor. 9-12
- ☐ 1 Cor. 13-16

Week 46
- ☐ 2 Cor. 1-3
- ☐ 2 Cor. 4-8
- ☐ 2 Cor. 9-11
- ☐ 2 Cor. 12-13
- ☐ Gal. 1-2
- ☐ Gal. 3-4
- ☐ Gal. 5-6

Week 47
- ☐ Eph.
- ☐ Phil.
- ☐ Col.
- ☐ 1 Thess.
- ☐ 2 Thess.
- ☐ 1 Tim.
- ☐ 2 Tim.

Week 48
- ☐ Titus - Philem.
- ☐ Heb. 1-6
- ☐ Heb. 7-10
- ☐ Heb. 11-13
- ☐ Jas.
- ☐ 1 Pet.
- ☐ 2 Pet.

Week 49
- ☐ 1 Jn. - 2 Jn.
- ☐ 3 Jn. - Jude
- ☐ Rev. 1-4
- ☐ Rev. 5-9
- ☐ Rev. 10-14
- ☐ Rev. 15-18
- ☐ Rev. 19-22

SMALL
GROUP
LEADERS

HOSTING AN OPEN HOUSE

If you're starting a new group, try planning an "open house" before your first formal group meeting. Even if you only have two to four core members, it's a great way to break the ice and to consider prayerfully who else might be open to joining you over the next few weeks. You can also use this kick-off meeting to hand out study guides, collect contact information for each person, ask for each person's birthday so you can later celebrate with them, spend some time getting to know each other, and briefly pray for each other.

A simple meal or good desserts always make a kick-off meeting more fun. After people introduce themselves and share how they ended up being at the meeting (you can play a game to see who has the wildest story!), have everyone respond to a few icebreaker questions: "What is your favorite family vacation?" or "What is one thing you love about your church/our community?" or "What are three things about your life growing up that most people here don't know?" Next, ask everyone to tell what he or she hopes to get out of the study. You might want to review the Small Group Agreement and talk about each person's expectations and priorities.

Finally, set an empty chair in the center of your group and explain that it represents someone who would enjoy or benefit from this group but who isn't here yet. Ask people to pray about whom they could invite to join the group over the next few weeks. Hand out postcards and have everyone write an invitation or two. Don't worry about ending up with too many people; you can always have one discussion circle in the living room and another in the dining room after you watch the lesson. Each group could then report prayer requests and progress at the end of the session.

You can skip this kick-off meeting if your time is limited, but you'll experience a huge benefit if you take the time to connect with each other in this way.

LEADING FOR THE FIRST TIME

- **Sweaty palms are a healthy sign.** The Bible says God is gracious to the humble. Remember who is in control; if you feel inadequate, that is probably a good sign. Those who are soft in heart (and sweaty palmed) are those whom God is sure to speak through.

- **Seek support.** Ask your leader, co-leader, or close friend to pray for you and prepare with you before the session. Walking through the study will help you anticipate potentially difficult questions and discussion topics.

- **Bring your uniqueness to the study.** Lean into who you are and how God wants you to uniquely lead the study.

- **Prepare.** Go through the lesson once before everyone arrives. Take time to listen to the teaching segment (DVD) and choose the questions you want to be sure to discuss.

- **Ask for feedback.** Perhaps in an email or on cards handed out at the study, have everyone write down three things you did well and one thing you could improve on.

- **Share with your group what God is doing in your heart.** God is searching for those whose hearts are fully His. Share your trials and victories. We promise that people will relate.

- **One final challenge:** Before your first opportunity to lead, look up each of the five passages listed below. Read each one as a devotional exercise to help equip yourself with a shepherd's heart. Trust us on this one. If you do this, you will be more than ready for your first meeting.

Matthew 9:36
1 Peter 5:2-4
Psalm 23
Ezekiel 34:11-16
1 Thessalonians 2:7-8, 11-12

LEADERSHIP TRAINING 101

Congratulations! You have responded to the call to help shepherd Jesus' flock. There are few other tasks in the family of God that surpass the contribution you will be making. As you prepare to lead, whether it is one session or the entire series, here are a few thoughts to keep in mind. We encourage you to read these and review them with each new discussion leader before he or she leads.

1   **Ask God for help.** Pray right now for God to help you build a healthy group. If you can enlist a co-leader you will find your experience to be much richer.

2   **Just be yourself.** Use your unique gifts and temperament. Don't try to do things exactly like another leader; do them in a way that fits you!

3   **Prepare for your meeting ahead of time.** Review the session and the leader's notes, and write down your responses to each question. Pay special attention to exercises that ask group members to do something other than engage in discussion. Review "Outline for Each Session" so you'll remember the purpose of each section in the study.

4   **Pray for your group members by name.** Before you begin your session, go around the room in your mind and pray for each member by name. You may want to review the prayer list at least once a week. Ask God to use your time together to touch the heart of every person uniquely. Expect God to lead you to whomever He wants you to encourage or challenge in a special way. If you listen, God will surely lead!

5   **When you ask a question, be patient.** Someone will eventually respond. Sometimes people need a moment or two of silence to think about the question; and if silence doesn't bother you, it won't bother anyone else. After someone responds, affirm the response with a simple "thanks" or "good point." Then ask, "How about somebody else?" or "Would someone who hasn't shared like to add anything?" Be sensitive to new people or reluctant members who aren't ready to say, pray, or do anything. If you give them a safe setting, they will blossom over time.

6 **Provide transitions between questions.** When guiding the discussion, use the "READ ALOUD" paragraphs as transitions into the questions. Ask the group if anyone would like to read the paragraph. Don't call on anyone, but ask for a volunteer, and then be patient until someone begins. Be sure to thank the person who reads aloud. These paragraphs can also be used for a more rich discussion if your group wants to expand on what was just read.

NOTES

PASTOR ALLEN JACKSON

Allen Jackson is passionate about helping people become more fully devoted followers of Jesus Christ who respond to God's invitations for their life.

He has served World Outreach Church since 1981, becoming senior pastor in 1989. Under his leadership, WOC has grown to a congregation of over 15,000 through outreach activities, community events and worship services designed to share the Gospel.

Through Allen Jackson Ministries, his messages reach people across the globe — through television, radio, Sirius XM, and online streaming. His teachings are also available in published books and other resources. Jackson has spoken at pastors' conferences in the U.S. and abroad, and has been a featured speaker during Jerusalem's Feast of Tabernacles celebration for the Vision for Israel organization and the International Christian Embassy- Jerusalem. Allen Jackson Ministries coaches pastors around the world, writing and publishing small-group curriculum used in states across the US, as well as Israel, Guatemala, the Philippines, Bermuda, Mexico, the United Kingdom, and South Africa.

With degrees from Oral Roberts University and Vanderbilt University, and additional studies at Gordon-Conwell Theological Seminary and Hebrew University of Jerusalem, Jackson is uniquely equipped to help people develop a love and understanding of God's Word.

Pastor Jackson's wife, Kathy, is an active participant in ministry at World Outreach Church.

THREE-VOLUME SMALL GROUP VIDEO STUDY & GUIDE

THE WHITEBOARD BIBLE

The Bible tells a story, and these small group studies will help you more fully understand it. The three volumes of *The Whiteboard Bible* develop a twelve-point timeline that serves as the framework for all the characters and events in the Bible, beginning with Creation and concluding with Jesus' return.

For more from Allen Jackson—including sermons, books, and small group materials—visit:

allenjackson.com

CPSIA information can be obtained
at www.ICGtesting.com
Printed in the USA
LVHW012148010522
717194LV00003B/5